No Hope!

The Story of the Great Red River Raft

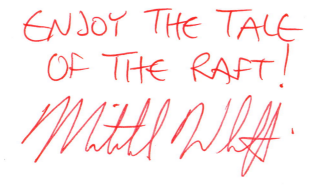

Mitchel Whitington

Copyright © 2009 by Mitchel Whitington

No part of this book may be reproduced or utilized in any form or by any means: electronic, mechanical or otherwise, including photocopying, recording or by any informational storage and retrieval system without permission in writing from the author.

Although the author has researched all sources to ensure the accuracy and completeness of the information contained within this book, no responsibility is assumed for errors, inaccuracies, omissions, or inconsistency herein. Any slights of people, places or organizations are completely and totally unintentional.

Works Cited and Footnote formats are based upon
the MLA Handbook, 6th ed., 2003.

ISBN
0-9801850-7-6 (10 digit)
978-0-9801850-7-2 (13 digit)

Library of Congress Catalog Number: 2009930219

First Edition

Printed in the United States of America
Published by 23 House Publishing
SAN 299-8084
www.23house.com

Cover photograph by R.B. Talfor, hand-colored by the photographer. Courtesy of the LSU-Shreveport Archives, Noel Memorial Library.

Dedication

Occasionally in life, you run across an individual who literally stuns you with the breadth of their knowledge on the subject of history. It doesn't take but a single conversation before you realize that the person has already forgotten more history than you'll ever know. Such a man was Fred McKenzie.

When his bookstore was on northeast Austin Street in Jefferson, I would go in to peruse the thousands of titles that he had there, and before long, we'd have struck up a conversation about some aspect of history, and an hour would have passed before I knew it. When he moved his shop to the old Black Swann building, he'd started carrying several of my books, so every few weeks I'd get a call to restock his inventory, and the visit would turn out to be the highlight of my day.

The city of Jefferson, Texas, lost a wonderful man in January of 2009. I was at his daughter's house the evening before the funeral, and it seemed like the entire town was there – laughing, talking, and telling stories about Fred's life. That man was truly loved by the citizens of Jefferson.

Out of all the things that Fred and I discussed over the few short years that I knew him, we never had the chance to talk about the Red River Raft. If we had, then this book might have been made better by his observations on the subject.

This book is therefore dedicated to the all the wonderful memories that I have of sitting in the chair across his desk and listening to the stories of that great author and historian, Fred McKenzie.

This one's for you, Fred – I hope that you would have liked it.

Table of Contents

Forward by the Author 1
The Origin of the Red River Raft 5
La Harpe's Exploration 1718-1720 21
The Dunbar-Hunter Expedition 1804-1805 26
The Freeman-Custis Expedition 1806 34
The Caddo Indians and the Raft 41
The Shreve Years 1832-1841 52
The Williamson Years 1842-1844 69
The Fuller Years 1850-1857 73
The Civil War and The Raft 1861-1865 81
The Final Taming of the Raft 1871-1873 87
Timeline of the Red River Raft 94
Bibliography – Books Cited 101
Bibliography – Periodicals Cited 106
Bibliography – Online Resources Cited 108
Bibliography – Government Resources Cited 109
Index 111

Forward by the Author

I first heard of the "Great Raft" over a decade ago when I was taking a tour in East Texas. The guide was describing how an unimaginable logjam on the red river – one that was over a hundred miles long – had shaped the terrain and waterways in Louisiana and Northeast Texas for centuries. It was interesting, and something that I'd never heard of before.

It didn't cross my mind again until several years later when my wife and I were vacationing in St. Francisville, Louisiana, and we returned to our B&B for the evening and turned on the History channel. A show was on about the New Madrid, Missouri earthquake that took place in the early 1800s, and among all the other havoc that it caused, the program credited it with creating the Red River Raft. Remembering what the tour guide had said, Tami and I talked about it for a minute, and then moved on with the show that we were watching.

After authoring many books on folklore, lighthearted history, and other topics, about a year ago I was working on one that brought the Raft back onto my radar scope. I started researching it in earnest, and became fascinated with the subject. I could find no one work that told its entire story, but more than that, I discovered quite a bit of conflicting information. The historian – and amateur sleuth – in me took over, and I set aside other projects to focus on the true story of the Great Red River Raft.

The results of that foray into Raft history became this book. I wanted to do a true, academic work, backed up by facts and footnotes. I know that some parts may be a little dry or dull, but by the time that you have finished reading it, I hope that you have an appreciation and understanding of how much the Great Raft shaped this part of the country over the years... and I sincerely hope that you enjoy the journey as much as I have.

There are other stories included in this book that could have gone untold. For example – and as I writer I don't want to give away any surprises – but the New Madrid earthquakes did not create the Raft. Still, because those quakes are so heavily entrenched in Raft lore, I included a good bit of information about them to show why people thought them to be responsible.

It's much the same thing with the Caddo Indians – the Raft's influence on them was long over toward the end of their history in the region, but I couldn't just let their story drop. I had to finish the brief look at their saga that I'd started.

For the side trips and extra information, please grant me a little leniency. It was a fun and informative journey for me, and I hope that it will be for you as well.

No Hope! The Story of the Great Red River Raft was an exciting – and sometimes frustrating – journey. Sifting through facts and piles of research material seemed like a daunting task, but it was made much easier by the people who helped along the way. They provided ideas, opinions, material, books, articles, illustrations and photographs for the book. This work would not have been possible without them. In no particular order, I would like to thank the following people for their time and assistance:

Ms. Laura Lyons McLemore, Ph.D. C.A., of the Noel Memorial Library at Louisiana State University-Shreveport was instrumental in helping me get permission to use the actual

Forward by the Author

photographs of the Great Raft that are shown in this book. I am so very grateful for them.

Richard Lay of St. Louis' Bellefontaine Cemetery was kind enough to provide me with a photograph of Captain Shreve's final resting place. As much as I'm looking forward to another trip to St. Louis (and some of their wonderful barbecue), I wasn't going to be able to make it before the book was released, so they helped me out with the photo. Now if I could only convince them to send me some of their barbecue!

Jerry Bloomer and the R.W. Norton Art Gallery were both very kind to grant me permission to reproduce Lloyd Hawthorne's painting of *Captain Henry M. Shreve Clearing the Great Raft from Red River, 1833-38*. It is an iconic work, and one that I'm thankful and honored to be able to include.

Ed Williams, Tim Richardson, and the Early Arkansaw Re-enactors Association gave me the photograph of their Dunbar-Hunter Expedition keelboat encampment. These folks help to preserve history by re-enacting it, and you can see their excursions on their website: http://www.arkie.net/~eara/ – the past truly comes alive there.

Diane Mallstrom, Reference Librarian, from the Public Library Of Cincinnati and Hamilton County helped me to secure permission to use the photograph of the New Falls City steamship in this book – that boat has an interesting story, and she came to *quite* an entertaining end.

I'd also be remiss if I didn't acknowledge the Library of Congress Archives and the Army Corps of Engineers Archives, both of which graciously allowed their photographs to be used. Both organizations do tremendous things to preserve our national history, and I commend them for their continuing efforts.

Finally, I have to give many thanks to my personal team that make this book a reality: Leonard and Betty Whitington, Ann Tillman, and as always, my wife Tami Whitington.

It always makes me nervous to go through and name the

people who helped with one of my books, because I'm sure that I'm going to miss someone. If I did in this case, I apologize profusely – I promise you that it was unintentional!

Some of the items in the book are public domain illustrations and photographs, and if I knew the correct people to thank for them from all those years ago when they were created, I would.

But finally, I have to give a genuine thanks to you, the reader, who is beginning the journey of discovering the Great Red River Raft. It is for you that this book was written, and I honestly hope that you enjoy it.

All that said, let's get on with the story, because I'm anxious to share it with you...

The Origin of the Red River Raft

It was formidable and impenetrable… a behemoth of logs blocking the Red River as far as the eye could see, stretching for over one hundred miles. The logjam – dubbed the "Red River Raft" – choked the river and denied passage there. It was so immense that when explorer Thomas Freeman first saw it, he penned in his journal, "No hope can be entertained of the great raft ever being removed…"[1]

While other North American rivers opened the continent up to exploration, settlement, and trade, the logjam made the Red impassible.

The massive logjam was further described by Freeman, who journaled: "The raft…consists of the trunks of large trees, lying in all directions, and damming up the river for its whole width, from the bottom, to about three feet higher than the surface of the water. The wood lies so compact that…large bushes, weeds and grass cover the surface of the raft…"[2] In fact, it was noted that the raft was so thick that the river "passes

---

[1] McCall, Edith. "The Attack on the Great Raft." American Heritage Magazine. Volume 3, Issue 3. Winter 1988.
[2] Muncrief, Dennis. "The Great Red River Raft." Oklahoma Genealogy & History. 5 January 2005. <http://www.okgenweb.org/~okmurray/Murray/stories/great_red_river_raft.htm>.

under this mass as if it were a bridge."[3]

Over the course of its history, the Red River Raft greatly influenced the lives of countless people: the Caddo Indians, the Spanish, the French, the Americans, Yankees, Confederates, and then the world of Reconstruction after the Civil War. As the history of the Red River region developed, the one constant, the one unconquerable force, was the incredible raft on the Red River.

The Great Red River Raft, courtesy of the
LSU-Shreveport Archives, Noel Memorial Library

Its beginnings are shrouded in mystery, and its slow demise spanned the lives of many brave pioneers dedicated to the task of clearing the massive logjam.

Several theories exist on the origin of the Raft. The first one has as its basis a series of earthquakes that took place in

---

[3] "The Red River Raft." The Manufacturer and Builder. Vol. IV, No. 1, January 1872.

New Madrid, Missouri, from December of 1811 through February of 1812. The most violent three of these measured 8.0 on the Richter Scale.[4]

These quakes were felt strongly over an area of 50,000 square miles, and could be detected across one million square miles of the United States. For a perspective on how massive this was, the great San Francisco earthquake of 1906 was felt moderately over only 6,000 square miles. Where the San Francisco earthquake was detected 350 miles away in Nevada, the New Madrid earthquakes rang church bells in Boston, Massachusetts some 1,000 miles away.[5]

Woodcutting from the 1800s showing the New Madrid Earthquake

---

[4] U.S. Geological Survey. "The Mississippi Valley – Whole Lotta Shakin' Goin' On." <http://quakes.usgs.gov/prepare/factsheets/NewMadrid>.
[5] ibid.

According to the U.S. Geological Survey, "Survivors reported that the earthquakes caused cracks to open in the earth's surface, the ground to roll in visible waves, and large areas of land to sink or rise. The crew of the *New Orleans* – the first steamboat on the Mississippi, which was on her maiden voyage – reported mooring to an island only to awake in the morning and find that it had disappeared below the waters of the Mississippi River. Damage was reported as far away as Charleston, South Carolina, and Washington, D.C."[6]

So violent were the rumblings that the very course of the mighty Mississippi River was altered, and the violent rolling of the land made parts of it flow backwards for a short time.[7]

The rivers in the region were certainly affected by the event. Captain John Davis of Natchez gave the following account of the earthquake while on the Mississippi River:

We arrived at night on the 15th December, 1811, at Island 25, and on the 16th at 2 a.m., we were surprised by the greatest commotion of the boat, which I could compare to nothing more than of a team of horses running away with a wagon over the most rocky road in our part of the country. There were forty flat-boats, barges and keel-boats in the company, and each thought his boat adrift and running over the sawyers; but a man on board a boat lashed to us hinted it to be an earthquake. An old navigator of the river just above, hailed us and said it was occasioned by the banks falling in. We were under a bluff bank which immediately cast off and fell in about a quarter of a mile, which drew us into the current on the right side of the island, where we staid till day; but in the meantime, we experienced fifty partial shocks, which shook our boat with great agitation. At 7 o'clock we heard a tremendous distant noise, and in a few seconds the boats, island and main land

---

[6] ibid.
[7] Feldman, Jay. When the Mississippi Ran Backwards. New York: Simon and Schuster, 2005.

became perfectly convulsed, the trees twisted and lashed together, the earth in all quarters was sinking, and the water issued from the center of Island 25, just on our left, and came rushing down its side in torrents. The shocks at this time became more frequent, one every fifteen minutes. The water rose from the first shock till about 8 o'clock that day eight feet perpendicular, and the current ran seven or eight miles an hour, as we ran from Island 25 and landed on Flower Island, a distance of thirty-five miles in five hours and twenty-five minutes. The logs, which had sprung up from the bottom of the river, were so thick that it appeared almost impossible for a boat to find a passage. There were a large number of boats sunk and destroyed, among them two boats of Mr. Jas. Atwell, of Kentucky. The logs and roots we passed had the sand and mud on them, which probably for many years lay in the bottom of the river, and which gave the appearance of timbered fields. We experienced shocks of earthquake for eight days. The whole country from the mouth of the Ohio to the White River country felt the terrible effects of this earthquake for many years — as many persons, houses and cattle were drowned or swallowed up by the opening of the earth. There were also several islands that disappeared, and many flat-boats and barges were wrecked. The town of New Madrid was a complete wreck and many of the people lost their lives. Our barge escaped and we arrived at Natchez, Jan. 5th, 1812.[8]

    As violent as the earthquake was, it isn't hard to imagine that it could have felled trees up and down the Red River, sending them tumbling into the river. When the waters were suddenly bombarded with huge tree trunks from a hundred miles of bank, the river's current could easily have melded the wood into a singular mass, which some say formed the basis for the Great Raft. Accounts such as this specifically attribute

---

[8] Gould, E.W. <u>Fifty Years on the Mississippi.</u> St. Louis: Nixon-Jones Printing, 1889.

the formation of the logjam to that New Madrid Earthquake.[9]

As plausible as this theory might be, however, facts firmly indicate that the Raft was in existence long before the ground began to shake in New Madrid, Missouri. As previously noted, the Freeman and Custis Red River Expedition documented the massive logjam in 1806, five years before the earthquake.[10]

Documentation of the Raft predates the Freeman and Custis exploration by almost a century, however. In 1718, the Company of the Indies commissioned Jean-Baptiste Bénard de La Harpe to explore the Louisiana area, and establish a trading post on the Red River. He traveled up the Red from Natchitoches, and reached "very difficult logjams" on his second day of travel.[11]

The Great Raft also appears on a map that was drawn in 1722 by a cartographer named J.F. Broutin. On his *Carte des Natchitoches*, or "map of Natchitoches," a segment of the raft is shown immediately above the Cane River area, which was a primary channel of the Red River at the time.[12]

So while it is certain that the Raft existed long before the New Madrid earthquakes, and they were not responsible for the forming of the Raft, there is some speculation that it could have been caused by another natural catastrophe… something that has occasionally happened in the eons of Earth's past.

The second theory of the origin of the Great Raft is one put forward by scientist, Near Earth Object researcher, and author E.P. Grondine, who suggests that the falling of the trees that formed the initial basis of the raft could have been due to something more cosmic. He hypothesizes that an impact event

---

[9] Moran, Nathan K. Earthquakes: Myths and Social Impacts. Memphis: The University of Memphis Press, 2008.
[10] McCall, op.cit.
[11] Carter, Cecile Elkins. Caddo Indians: Where We Come From. Norman: University of Oklahoma Press, 2001.
[12] Bagur, Jacques D. A History of Navigation on Cypress Bayou and the Lakes. Denton: University of North Texas Press, 2001.

– when an asteroid or comet hits the surface of the Earth, for example – could have occurred as early as 700 A.D.[13]

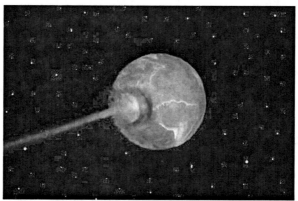

Portrayal of an Impact Event on Earth

He supports his theory not only from speculation as to the condition of the wood remnants of the raft, but also by the movement of indigenous people from the area. The Troyville culture of Louisiana Indians existed approximately from 400-800 A.D., after which time it came to an abrupt end. It is possible that an impact event caused the demise of this culture, with survivors moving further north in to the area that would eventually become Arkansas. Many years after the natural disaster, the Louisiana region became populated by the Indians of the Coles Creek culture. Grondine speculates that specific proof of the event could be found if remnants from an atmospheric blast could be excavated in the area, or if the remains of flash-burned trees in remnants of the Great Raft could be located.[14]

---

[13] Grondine, E.P. "Everything is Connected: Searching for Historical Impacts in North America and a Survey of Southern and Eastern Native American Sites." Cambridge Conference Correspondence. 4 September 2000.
[14] Ibid.

With all that said, the third – and generally accepted – theory is that the driftwood accumulations began at the mouth of the Red River as result of higher water levels in the Mississippi River. This is described in an 1855 article that was published in a periodical called *DeBow's Review*:

At what time it [the Red River Raft] commenced is unknown and must remain so; but, judging from its annual decay, breaking off and floating away below, gives probability to the conjecture that it was more than four hundred years ago. The Caddo Indians say that the residence of their immediate ancestors was on Caddo prairie, now the bottom of the present Caddo lake, and this at the upper end of the obstruction. This open lake, about one and a half miles in width and thirty or forty long, is about eight feet in depth under general winter water and passway for steamboats. When the raft was first seen by the earliest white settlers is and will also remain unknown. When Alexandria and Natchitoches, one hundred miles above it, were first settled, the raft was above them, and this latter Spanish town was founded as early as the city of Philadelphia. When operations were commenced by the United States engineers, in 1833, under Captain Shreeve [SIC], its lower end was at the mouth of the Loggy Bayou, which is the outlet of Lakes Bodeau and Bistmon, and near four hundred miles above the mouth of the river and the commencement of the obstruction, all below having rotted and passed away. We are not in so much doubt, however, how the raft was first created. The cause, it seems generally agreed, was, that the waters of the Mississippi being high from a freshet when the Red River was low, its waters backed up and made still-water at its mouth. The rafts of trees, logs and drift that came down the Red river were stopped by the ceasing of its current in this still-water, and spread over the surface from bank to bank and there accumulated. When the Mississippi water fell, all this accumulated drift over so much surface, seeking passage out at the same time, united and tangled from shore to shore and stopped and made a jam. The mass of imbedded logs near the mouth and very many places above, that show themselves in low states of the river, make this certain. The jam once established, as nothing could pass, increased each year according as the extent of the annual freshets brought down more trees and drift, and this accumulation probably was at about the rate of one and a half miles a year, while after a time from decay it broke away below, drifted off and made a clear river at something like the average of about one-half that space. When surveyed for the operations that were begun in 1833, its length was a little under one hundred and thirty miles. Since 1833 it has extended to about thirty miles above where it ended at that time. The sap woods of the swamp under the alternations of wet and dry were not many years in rotting, and when completely rotted broke away and past down the stream so as to make again an open river. The annual increase, exceeding the decrease, gave length to it and advanced it into the upper country; and if these were the days of M. Van Winkle, and we would wait about two hundred years, it would give us navigation up to Fulton, near the natural obstruction known as the White Oak Shoals, and about eight hundred miles above its mouth.[15]

The obstruction known as the Great Raft effectively blocked all traffic on the river. Since the Red was fed by smaller rivers, creeks, swamps and adjoining lakes, it was sometimes possible for travelers to use these adjunct waterways as a network of passageways to navigate around the raft. Such a task was extremely slow and laborious, however. Navigation of these other waterways often depended on factors such as the season, the amount of rainfall, etc.

In 1819, a traveler named W.B. Dewees penned a letter to a friend describing his voyage up the Red River, including an

---

[15] DeBow, J.D.B., "Red River Raft." Debow's Review Vol. XIX. – New Series, Vol. II. 1855.

interesting description of the logjam that he encountered there:
Long Prairie, Ark., March 1, 1819
My Dear Friend:

Agreeably to promise, I take this the first opportunity to give you a description of my travels, since I left my home in Kentucky. I took water on board a large keel boat at Nashville, Tennessee. We sailed down the Cumberland River, into the Ohio, and thence into the Mississippi. This part of the voyage occupied about a week. The scenery on the banks of the Cumberland is very pleasant. There are but few villages on this river, and these few are small. The most important is Smithland, situated at the mouth of the river. It probably contains about two hundred inhabitants. As I did not stop in this place, I am unable to give you a description of it. After leaving the Cumberland River, we proceeded down into the Mississippi; on this river there are but few inhabitants. Most of them were pale-faced, sickly looking people, apparently fishermen and wood-choppers. After traveling about a week on this river, we arrived at a place called Chickasaw Bluffs. This is a small village, containing some ten or fifteen inhabitants. About three days after leaving the Chickasaw Bluffs, we reached the Walnut Hills, on the east bank of the river. We could see these hills at about the distance of two miles. They are elevated seventy-five or one hundred feet above the common level of the river. Although it was in the winter season, the grass was perfectly green. The scenery was certainly enchanting! I wish you could see them! I know you would be delighted. Oh! That I had the pencil of a painter, or the pen of a poet, that I might give you a description of these charming hills! The country surrounding these hills is covered with a thick growth of timber. From the midst of the timber rise these hills covered with a carpet of richest green. Indeed I could think of nothing but our old Kentucky wheat fields.

After leaving the Walnut Hills, we saw nothing worthy of note until we reached Natchez. Here we remained about a

The Origin of the Red River Raft

week. Natchez is a very beautiful town, situated on a high bluff, except a small portion of it, which is on the bank of the river, under a hill. I have often heard of dissipation, but I never saw it in its nakedness till I came to this place. It would fill you with perfect horror, were I to describe to you the fighting which is carried on between the boatmen and the citizens of "Natchez under the hill." Indeed my pen would fail in the description of it. No one can conceive the horrors of this place unless they themselves have witnessed the scenes. Here you might see men, women, and children mingling together in every species of vice and dissipation; the very thoughts of which is enough to sicken the heart.

The vessels upon this river consist in part of barges and keel boats; but mostly of upper country flat boats, (generally called broad-horns,) and chicken thieves. With these you are already familiar, and a description is unnecessary. But while at Natchez I saw a steamboat. I spent some time on board examining this boat. I wish I could convey an adequate description of this craft. It is, as you of course know, propelled by steam, and moves through the water with great rapidity. I think this invention of Robert Fulton will eventually prove to be of great advantage to this part of the country, and I hope the time will soon come, as I firmly believe it will, when they take the place of the vessels which are now occupied in navigating this majestic river. Nor do I think I am too sanguine when I say that in twenty-five years from now, whoever lives to see that time, will find steam navigation to be the most common mode.

After leaving Natchez, we proceeded down the Mississippi to the mouth of the Red River. On this part of our journey we saw a few large plantations. The banks of the river below Natchez are much more thickly inhabited than above. The scenery on the banks of the river is truly delightful, but I did not much like the looks of the river itself, it has such a dirty, turbid look. True, I was prepared to expect this, but for all that I was disappointed. I did not like to think that our most noble stream presented such an unpleasant appearance. But so we ever find it in this life! It is not the most beautiful that is the most noble; nor is it always in the fairest countenance that we find the most ennobling qualities of the heart.

After entering Red River, we found our labors very toilsome; on account of our boat being a large, family boat, crowded with women and children, we found it very difficult to row and push up stream. However, we got along very well, though slowly, until we arrived at the Big Raft. On our way we passed the thriving towns of Alexandria and Natchitoches. At Alexandria we were detained about four days in rigging a windlass to pull our boat over the Rapids. These Rapids are a ledge of rocks running across the river, over which the water falls perpendicularly to the depth of three feet.

The coast of Red River from the mouth up to Alexandria is inhabited mostly by Creole French. Some of these are very wealthy planters. The land is very rich, producing cotton and sugar in great abundance.

Our course through the raft was very slow and toilsome. The distance is about ninety miles. We were thirty days in making this distance. Ours is the only boat of any size that has ever passed through the raft. Had we not been fortunate as to secure the service of a Caddo Indian, who had passed through before, as a guide, we should likely have been lost.

I hardly know how to give you a description of this raft, but perhaps you can get the best idea of it by imagining yourself in a large swamp, grown up with trees and filled up with driftwood, wedged in very closely, the water having no particular current and running in no particular direction. During the thirty days we saw land but two or three times, and then only some small islands. At night we tied our boats to a tree and remained till morning. Sometimes we would come across lakes two or three miles in extent, and then again we would spend a whole day in moving not further than the length of the boat.

The Origin of the Red River Raft

But I must not forget to tell you of the immense quantity of bee trees which we found in this raft. At any time we could go in our "dug out," and return laden with a large quantity of honey, which we found truly delicious.

While passing through the raft a circumstance of melancholy interest took place. A Mrs. Reddeford, from Tennessee, one night when we were all asleep, went out upon the running boards and fell overboard. The sound of her falling awoke some one of the boat's company who instantly gave the alarm. A young man and myself ran immediately to the stern of the boat and saw her rise. We plunged into the water and swam to the place where we saw her rise, just then she rose again a few yards below. We swam to that place and by reaching down I felt her hair floating in the water. With the assistance of my friend I swam with her to the boat. She was apparently lifeless, but by laying her stomach on a flour-barrel and rolling it, we succeeded in bringing her to life. Since then there has been a strange, wild look about her eyes, though she is now perfectly well.

After we were safely through the raft, we had no difficulty in getting to this place, which is only lit a three days' journey. The country from Natchitoches to this place is generally uninhabited, except by a few Indians. The bottom is heavily timbered, large cane brakes, and mostly low rich land.

Perhaps there is nothing that strikes the eye of a Kentuckian with more surprise than the long moss hanging from the branches of the trees. This pendant parasite as it sways to and fro in the wind gives to the landscape a peculiarly melancholy and somber appearance, and frequently it even darkens the air.

On the banks of this river there are a great quantity of very large alligators, which, by the by, are very dangerous, as they frequently drown dogs, horses and even men.

Long Prairie is the first large prairie on Red river, from the mouth up. It bluffs to the river, runs back fifteen or twenty miles, and is surrounded by a heavily timbered country. The land is very rich. At the present time, the prairie is covered with a carpet of rich verdure, here and there interspersed with beautiful wild flowers. The population of this part of the country consisted of two families previous to our arrival. As to the health of the place I know but little, having been here but a few days; but from appearances I should not judge favorably of it. Here I saw for the first time a person shaking with the ague. I supposed the person to be dying, but was told it was nothing but the ague.

I am expecting to leave this place in a few days for Mound Prairie, some one hundred and fifty miles further up the river, from which place I will write you again.
Till then adieu. Your affectionate friend,
W.B.D.[16]

Dewees' letter is an excellent example of the typical journey that a traveler on the Red River in 1819 could expect, and illustrates the difficulty that one would have traversing the area obstructed by the Raft. A few years later, a missionary named Timothy Flint described the Raft in the 1820s:

About thirty leagues above Natchitoches commences the Raft, which is nothing more than a broad swampy expansion of alluvion [SIC] of the river to the width of 20 or 30 miles. The river, spreading here into a vast number of channels, frequently shallow of course, has been for ages clogging with a compact mass of timber, and fallen trees wafted from the upper regions. Between these masses the river has a channel, sometimes lost in a lake, and found by following the outlet of that lake back to the parent channel. There is no state of water, in which a keel boat with an experienced pilot may not make her way through the raft. The river is blocked up by this immense mass of timber for a length, on its meanders, of

---

[16] Dewees, W.B. <u>Letters From an Early Settler of Texas</u>. Louisville: Hull & Brothers, 1854.

between 60 and 70 miles. There are places where the water can be seen in motion under the logs. In other places, the whole width of the river may be crossed on horseback, and boats only make their way, in passing these places, by following the inlet of a lake, and coasting it to its outlet, and thus finding the channel again. Weeds, flowering shrubs, and small willows have taken root upon the surface of this timber, and flourish above the waters. But in all these places the course of the river, its outline and its bends are distinctly marked by a margin of forest trees, which grow here on the banks in the same manner, as they do when the channel is open.[17]

Descriptions of the Raft as given above are not the only documentation of the massive logjam, however. It was known across the continent, and appears in many items of the time's popular culture.

Consider, for example, that in 1880, author John Habberton wrote a book titled *Romance of California Life* where the Raft is mentioned in casual dialog:

"*Reputation be hanged!*" *exclaimed Fred. "Lose it, for your wife's sake. Besides, you'll make reputation instead of lose it; you'll be as famous as the Red River Raft, or the Mammoth Cave – the only thing of the kind west of the Alleghanies.*"

Another example of the Raft's fame is shown in the following passage from the poem *Our Country* written by Henry David Thoreau in 1841:

It is a noble country where we dwell,
Fit for a stalwart race to summer in;
From Madawaska to Red River raft,
From Florid keys to the Missouri forks,
See what unwearied copious streams
Come tumbling to the east and southern shore...

---

[17] Bagur, op.cit.

No Hope! The Story of the Great Red River Raft

The story of the Great Raft begins, though, long before the United States existed, when the North American continent was raw and bountiful. European explorers were just starting to make their way into the new world, and some sailed into the Gulf of Mexico and started inland on the network of rivers. The Mississippi could be easily navigated, but when they ventured onto the Red, the adventurers soon encountered the huge obstruction that would come to be known as the Great Red River Raft.

La Harpe's Exploration 1718-1720

One of the first recorded accounts of the Red River Raft was given by French explorer Jean-Baptiste Bénard de La Harpe during his journey through Louisiana.

Born on February 4th, 1683 in Saint-Malo, France, he began a life of adventure at the age of eighteen by serving in the Spanish army of King Philip V as a cavalry officer. He completed his term there after only two years, and then returned to his hometown.[18] In 1703, La Harpe joined an exploration mission to Peru. There he met a woman twenty-two years his senior, a widow named Dona Maria de Rokafull, and the couple married. They returned to France in 1706, where La Harpe published a volume of his adventures titled *Relation*.[19]

Tragically, his wife died after three years, and he became embattled in a bitter lawsuit with her family over her riches. This lasted six years, and in 1715, the decision was finally handed down against him – he lost all claim to her fortune.[20]

La Harpe married once again, but she also died after only a

---

[18] Smith, Ralph A. "Account of the Journey of Benard de La Harpe: Discovery Made by Him of Several Nations Situated in the West." Southwestern Historical Quarterly, Vol. 62. July, 1958.
[19] Villiers du Terrage, Marc de. <u>An Explorer of Louisiana: Jean-Baptiste Bénard de la Harpe</u>. Arkadelphia: Institute for Regional Studies, Ouachita Baptist University, 1983.
[20] ibid.

few years. By then he had purchased two honorary titles there in France: Governor of the town of Dol, and Lieutenant General of the Brittany Coast Guard. Both titles that he bought were soon abolished, and having nothing to hold him in his country of birth, La Harpe left France in 1718.[21]

Along with forty other men, he set sail for the New World as part of Scottish financier John Law's desire to have a colony there. He sailed from Saint-Malo, France, and landed on Dauphin Island off the coast of North America, which is present-day Alabama.[22]

From there he proceeded to the French settlement of New Orleans, where he presented himself to Jean-Baptiste Le Moyne de Bienville, governor of the Louisiana colony. Bienville appointed him to be a concessionaire for the Company of the Indies, with orders to explore the Mississippi, Red, and Sulphur rivers, and to establish a northern trading post. He departed on December 17th, 1718.[23]

Woodcutting of La Harpe with his Indian guides

La Harpe arrived at the mouth of the Red River by January 10th, 1719 and proceeded northward. Due to his struggles with

---

[21] Smith, op.cit.
[22] ibid.
[23] ibid.

the rapids and the raft, it took him three months to travel to the Sulphur River with his heavily laden pirogues and flatboats.[24]

After only a week on the Red River, he recorded:

We found some timbers so thick that it seemed incredible to be able to go through them. There were on the branches of these trees an infinite number of snakes, upon which it was necessary for us to fire some musket shots from fear that they might fall into our boats. This route was very painful and fatigued our men extremely. We entered afterwards into a channel full of alligators where the currents were frightful. We passed through it by the tow line and by pulling ourselves from branch to branch.[25]

La Harpe managed to navigate around the logjam using the bayou system that fed the river, and continued to press northward. In April of that year he established Fort Saint Louis de los Cadodaquious on land that he purchased from the Nassonites Indians, a Caddoan tribe, in what is now Bowie County near Texarkana, Texas. La Harpe had hoped to establish a trading center there with both the Spanish and the Indians, but friction between the French and the Spanish in the War of the Quadruple Alliance kept the post from being a success.[26]

He continued his exploration of the Red River and the Sulphur River, passing through present-day Texas, Arkansas and Oklahoma. La Harpe is probably best remembered for the following legend:

In 1719...Bernard [SIC] de la Harpe pushed up the Red River from the tiny French outpost of Natchitoches and crossed the plains to a spot well along the upper course of the Arkansas. Two years later, urged by some strange Indian tales

---

[24] Wedel, Mildred Mott. La Harpe's 1719 Post on Red River and Nearby Caddo Settlements. Austin: Texas Memorial Museum, 1978.
[25] Carter, op.cit.
[26] Villiers du Terrage, op.cit.

of an emerald rock in the stream, he came up the Arkansas itself, sighting the first small outcropping of greenish-brown schist and sandstone where the city of Little Rock later was built on the south bank of the river, and giving it the name that has persisted to this day.[27]

La Harpe himself refuted this story – it was told not by the explorer himself, but by a member of his party some twenty years later. Still, the legend is forever commemorated in Emerald Park on the summit of "Big Rock" in the city of North Little Rock, and La Harpe's name has been given to the boulevard closest to the river in downtown Little Rock.

La Harpe's map of his explorations

In November 1719 he returned to the Red River, and traversing the Great Raft once again, he finally arrived back in New Orleans in January 1720. From there he returned to

---

[27] Fletcher, John Gould. Arkansas. Fayetteville: University of Arkansas Press, 1995.

France, disenchanted with his Red River experience.[28]

He would return to the New World for more experiences, some successful, some not, but in the course of his travels he wrote several accounts of his adventures. Many of his writings are considered to be either exaggerations or downright fiction by his peers at the time and historians of today, but the significant information about the difficulties of the time, the peoples that he encountered, and the terrain found on his journeys cannot be disputed.[29]

Jean-Baptiste Bénard de La Harpe died in his hometown of Saint-Malo on September 26th, 1765. History will remember him as one of the first persons to record an encounter with the great Red River Raft.

The Great Red River Raft, courtesy of the LSU-Shreveport Archives, Noel Memorial Library

---

[28] Smith, op.cit.
[29] Wedel, op.cit.

The Dunbar-Hunter Expedition 1804-1805

One of the cornerstones of Thomas Jefferson's presidential career was the Louisiana Purchase in 1803 – the U.S. acquisition of 828,800 acres of land from France for approximately $15,000,000.[30] Jefferson knew the importance of sending explorers into this new frontier to not only map the region, but also to report on settlements, Indian tribes, animals, vegetation, and the terrain. The most famous expedition was Lewis and Clark, who explored the Missouri River region from 1803 to 1806, and brought back invaluable information.

A much less famous excursion took place from 1804 to 1805 – the Dunbar-Hunter Expedition. President Jefferson felt that an exploration to survey the Arkansas and Red River watersheds would be extremely beneficial. He sent a letter to a scientist and acquaintance, William Dunbar of Natchez, Mississippi, and asked him to lead such a party. In the letter, Jefferson said:

Congress will probably authorize me to explore the greater waters on the Western side of Mississippi and Missouri, to their sources in case I should propose to send... another party up the Arcansa [SIC] to its source, thence that to

---

[30] Dennedy, David M.; Cohen, Lizabeth; and Bailey, Thomas A. <u>The American Pageant.</u> Florence: Wadsworth Publishing, 2001.

its mouth... These several surveys will enable us to prepare a map of Louisiana... as you live near the point of departure of the lowest expedition and can acquire so much better the information... I have thought if Congress should authorize the enterprize [SIC] to propose to you the unprofitable trouble of directing it.[31]

The President recommended a partner to Dunbar – Dr. George Hunter, a chemist and druggist with experience in wilderness exploration. Hunter had proven himself with the backcountry of Ohio and Indiana and seemed to be a perfect pairing for Dunbar. Specifically, President Jefferson wrote Dunbar that Dr. Hunter's "forte is chemistry, and in the practical part of that science he is supposed to have no equal in the United States." He did warn Dunbar, however, that Dr. Hunter might attempt to turn their assignment into a gold or silver hunting expedition, and that such a deviation should not be allowed.[32]

After Congress appropriated $3,000 for the expedition, intense planning for the trip began. After analyzing the situation, however, both Jefferson and Dunbar determined that tension with the Osage Indians might become problematic. Specifically, there was apprehension about a specific group of the Osage led by a chief named Great Track that had split away from the main tribe. Jefferson wrote Dunbar, saying he feared that Great Track and his Osage would not only impede the expedition, but "perhaps do worse." There was also a possibility of interference from the Spanish above Bayou Pierre off the Red River – since the boundary between America's Louisiana Purchase and the area still owned by Spain was in dispute, a U.S. expedition up the Red might be viewed as an

---

[31] Berry, Trey. "The Expedition of William Dunbar and George Hunter along the Ouachita River, 1804-1805." <u>Arkansas Historical Quarterly.</u> 1 January 2003.

[32] Cox, Isaac Joslin. "The Louisiana-Texas Frontier III." <u>Southwestern Historical Quarterly.</u> Volume 17, Number 2. October, 1913.

invasion.[33] The scope of operation was therefore changed to include travel up the Mississippi to the Red River, Black River, and then finally up the Ouachita as far as the reported "hot springs."[34]

Dunbar first wrote Jefferson about this change in plan in June of 1804. On August 18th, 1804, he contacted the President again to encourage acceptance of the new plan, stating that there were many "curiosities" along the Ouachita River, specifically referring to the location that he called "the boiling springs or fountain."[35]

Jefferson approved, and on October 16th, 1804, the expedition launched from St. Catherine's Landing near the city of Natchez on the east bank of the Mississippi River. They used a "strange-looking 'Chinese-style vessel' that had been designed by Hunter in Pittsburgh several months earlier. The party was comprised of Dunbar and Hunter, Hunter's son, three of Dunbar's slaves, and thirteen enlisted soldiers.[36]

The odd boat proved to be impractical for river travel, and cost the party a month's travel time.[37] It was therefore exchanged for a much more practical flatboat when the party reached Fort Miro, or Ouachita Post, which is now the city of Monroe, Louisiana. The old French city that had been established in 1784 had been converted to American control in April of 1804.

Dunbar and Hunter kept extensive diaries of the journey and the wildlife and flora that they encountered. In their journey up the Red River, the expedition encountered the Red River Raft, as chronicled by Dunbar:

The Red and Arcansas [SIC] rivers whose countries are

---

[33] Berry, op.cit.
[34] Dunbar, William. Journal of a Voyage... to the Mouth of the Red River. Philadelphia: American Philosophical Society, 1809.
[35] Berry, op.cit.
[36] ibid.
[37] Cox, op. cit.

very long, pass thro' portions of this fine Country, they are both navigable to an unknown distance by boats of proper construction. the Arcansas river is however understood to have greatly the advantage over its neighbour with respect to the facility of navigation: some difficult places are met in the Red River below the Nakitosh, after which it is good for 150 leagues (probably the computed leagues of the Country of nearly two miles each) there the Voyager meets with a very serious obstance, viz the commencement of the Raft as it is called, that is, a natural covering which conceals the whole river for an extent of 17 leagues continually augmenting by the drift wood, supports at this time a vegetation of every thing abounding in the neighbouring forest, not excepting trees of considerable size, and the river may be frequently passed with any knowledge of its existence; it is said that the annual inundation is opening for itself a new passage thro' the low grounds near the hills, but it must be a long time before nature unaided will dig out a passage sufficient for the reception of the waters of the Red River; about 50 leagues above the natural bridge is the residence of the Cadeaux or Cadadoquis Nation, of whose good qualities we have already spoken; the inhabitants estimate the Post of Nakitosh to be half way between New Orleans and the Cadeaux Nation.[38]

The expedition continued on to the mouth of the Black River, and then up the Ouachita. On November 15th, 1804, they crossed into what would become modern-day Arkansas.

As they reached the city of Encore a Fabri, which is Camden, Arkansas today, two very interesting things happened. Dunbar and Hunter encountered a tree trunk that was carved with interesting Indian hieroglyphs consisting of human and animal figures. One scene depicted two persons

---

[38] Dunbar, William; Hunter, George; Berry, Trey; Beasley, Pam; and Clements, Jeanne. The Forgotten Expedition, 1804-1805. Baton Rouge: Louisiana State University Press, 2006.

holding or shaking hands, leading them to believe that it could have been the site of trade between the Indians and Europeans. The second thing that occurred was that on November 22nd, Hunter was cleaning his pistol and the gun discharged. The bullet tore through two fingers and his thumb, and missed his head by inches – it tore through the brim of his hat. He was wounded and in constant pain for several weeks; his eyes were powder-burned, and he could not see nor write. For a period of time, Dr. Hunter became a burden to the expedition – he was no use in recording the things that they encountered.[39]

As they continued on, many changes were observed. The trees became "birch, maple, holly, ironwood, dogwood, ash and sweet gum… white black and red oak."[40]

The Dunbar-Hunter Expedition keelboat encampment, as re-created by the Early Arkansaw Re-enactors Association in 2007, courtesy of the Early Arkansaw Re-enactors Association, photograph by Tim Richardson

When they reached the settlement that in today's world is Arkadelphia, Arkansas, they encountered a Dutch man named Paltz who had lived on the Ouachita River for forty years.

---

[39] ibid.
[40] ibid.

When the group asked for information about any interesting places in the area, Paltz directed them to a salt pit. With his eyes healed, Dr. Hunter conducted scientific tests on the saline water there, and determined it to be "marine salt."[41]

On December 3rd, 1804, the group reached the area that is now Malvern in Hot Spring County, and encountered a series of rapids and boulders on the Ouachita River that stretched for almost a mile. Dunbar described the rapids and rock formations in his writing as looking like "ancient fortifications and castles."[42] They rocked the boat from side to side, and basically dragged it through the maze of boulders.

The group managed to pass, however, and by December 7th they had reached the closest point along the Ouachita River to the hot springs, and they camped at the confluence of a creek they identified as Calfait Creek. As several of the men could not wait to see the famed "boiling springs," several men immediately began a nine-mile walk to examine the site. They returned the next afternoon with vivid descriptions of their experiences, stating that they had discovered an empty cabin thought to be used by those coming to bathe in and drink from the reported healing waters of the springs.

The Dunbar and Hunter expedition began an almost four-week study of the water properties and geological and biological features that were there. Along with cataloging the hot springs, the explorers spotted animals such as swans, deer, raccoons, and buffalo around their camp and in the area of the hot springs. As 1804 came to an end, temperatures began to fall, and after a snowstorm Dunbar decided that it was time to return home. Although both leaders of the expedition wanted to be able to explain the source of the hot water, they left the area on January 8th, 1805 with only speculations.[43]

---

[41] ibid.
[42] ibid.
[43] Berry, op.cit.

The expedition made the trip back in less than half the time that it had taken to reach the hot springs. They stopped briefly at Fort Miro so that Hunter could retrieve his Chinese-style boat. Dunbar, traveling with a servant, reached his home in Natchez on January 26th; Hunter and the rest of the party arrived on January 27th. After an evening's rest, Hunter and his son took their Chinese boat to New Orleans, and then returned to Philadelphia via New York.[44]

Both Dunbar and Hunter began to work on their respective reports to Jefferson. Unfortunately, the explorers could not report anything of great significance. The natural hot springs that had been the culmination of their journey was a natural curiosity, but the seasons of their travels were unfavorable for any extensive botanical observations. Both of the reports would reach the President's desk a full year before Lewis and Clark's. Dunbar's journals, followed by Hunter's, gave Jefferson a glimpse, albeit a limited one, into the Louisiana Purchase wilderness.

Dr. Hunter gave an interview to the *New Orleans Gazette* on February 14th, 1805, where he extolled the virtues and opportunities that waited in the areas that the party had explored. He also presented the potential healing properties of the hot springs that they had encountered.[45]

Both Dunbar and Hunter expected that they would start assembling their next journey – the "Grand Expedition" – later that same year. Congress did not appropriate the funds for this next mission, and the two men gave up on the dream and resumed their normal lives.

President Jefferson used the two men's journals as part of a presentation to Congress about the Louisiana Purchase, and in 1806 an account of their travels was published in a work entitled *Message from the President of the United States*

---

[44] ibid.
[45] ibid.

Communicating Discoveries Made in Exploring the Missouri, Red River and Washita[SIC].[46]

Although the Dunbar-Hunter expedition did not explore the length of the Red River that was originally intended, they were able to provide a detailed description of the hot springs area of the Ouachita River, and gave an account of the Red River Raft as they encountered it in 1804.

The Great Red River Raft – note the man standing in the middle of the river, courtesy of the LSU-Shreveport Archives, Noel Memorial Library

---

[46] ibid.

The Freeman-Custis Expedition 1806

In 1805, Jefferson was ready for a full expedition up the Red River. Both Dunbar and Hunter had returned to their normal lives, so neither wanted to lead it. Instead, he chose Thomas Freeman, a cartographer who had accompanied Andrew Ellicott on the survey of the U.S. southern boundary; Dr. Peter Custis, a naturalist and botanist; and Captain Richard Sparks to represent the military. Lieutenant Humphrey, a man "of considerable talents," was appointed to be Freeman's assistant. The final party was finally assembled: Freeman and Custis, Humphrey, Sparks, two additional military officers, seventeen privates, along with a servant – twenty-four in all.[47]

On April 19th, 1806, the party left Fort Adams in two flat-bottom barges and a pirogue and headed up the Red on a journey of discovery. One month later they reached Natchitoches, where they stopped for two weeks to re-supply. At the time, this was the last American settlement on the river.[48]

Freeman and Custis met John Sibley there, who was the American Indian Agent for the region. He supplied additional trade goods, so that the members of the expedition could obtain

---

[47] Cox, Isaac Joslin. "The Freeman Red River Expedition." <u>Proceedings of the American Philosophical Society, Vol. 92, No. 2, Studies of Historical Documents in the Library of the American Philosophical Society.</u> Philadelphia: American Philosophical Society, 5 May 1948.
[48] ibid.

horses from the Ouachita Indians upriver. The expedition took on more soldiers at that point because of rumors of unrest between the Spanish and the United States. This brought their number up to thirty-seven men. The explorers left Natchitoches on June 2nd.[49]

In 1948, Isaac Joslin Cox summarized the expedition in his writings for the American Philosophical Society:

Above Natchitoches, which they left June 2, the river continued its divided course. In fact its waters, for about 100 miles, were dispersed in a series of bayous, lakes and swamps, through which there was no single channel. At certain seasons much of this land was flooded. Here the explorers encountered the "Great Raft," then, and for many years to come, impassable for craft of any sort. A local guide conducted them through a tributary bayou which, like its fellow branches, seemed to leave and enter the main stream at will. These bayous and the lakes that they joined, varied in length and depth, but were frequently bordered by bluffs, which rose to some height above the immediate banks. The latter at that time were some 15 to 20 feet above the surface of the water. Occasionally one channel might maintain for some distance a width of 150 to 200 yards and then narrow to half that distance. Cypress and hardwoods, cedar, cottonwoods, and other forest trees were interspersed with numerous varieties of shrubs and flowers and stretches of grassy and timber-covered slopes that gave variety to the landscape, where it was visible, but rendered progress through this watery maze difficult on account of numerous rafts and at times dangerous from the falling of dead trees. These often crashed upon a slight impact from the passing boat. Frequently there seemed no passage whatever between the standing tree trunks. The party took two weeks to navigate this formidable detour of 98 miles, before their craft floated once more on the undivided river. They had

---

[49] ibid.

been warned against attempting the passage with such craft and were correspondingly elated at their progress.[50]

Freeman himself recorded, "After fourteen days of incessant fatigue, toil, and danger, doubt and uncertainty, we at length gained the river above the Great Raft, contrary to the decided opinion of every person who had any knowledge of the difficulties we had to encounter."[51]

The following excerpt from Thomas Freeman's journal further describes their encounter with several sections of the Great Raft:

The first raft is not more than 40 yards through. It consists of the trunks of large trees, lying in all directions, and damming up the river for its whole width, from the bottom, to about three feet higher than the surface of the water. The wood lies so compact that large bushes, weeds and grass cover the surface of the raft. The party encamped on the evening of the seventh...

Next morning we came to the second raft, which crosses the river here 100 feet in width, and extends for 200 yards along its course. This raft rises nearly three feet above the water, and is covered with bushes and weeds: the trees of which it is composed are Cotton Wood, Cypress, Red Cedar, etc, and they lie so close that the men could walk over it in any direction. With great exertions we opened a passage for the boats, through this raft on one side, by floating the large trees down the river...

On the even of the ninth we arrived as the third raft, like the two former, composed of the trunks of trees, brought down by the floods, and lodges on sand bars; forming an almost impenetrable mass, which extends from the bottom of the river, to two or three feet above the surface of the water, a thickness

---

[50] ibid.
[51] Allen, John Logan. <u>North American Exploration: A Continent Comprehended.</u> Lincoln: University of Nebraska Press, 1997.

of 30 or 40 feet. This raft extends up the river nearly 300 yards. Many of these logs were of Red Cedar, from 1 to 3 feet in diameter, and 60 feet in length. With much difficulty a passage was effected through this; as the vacancy, occasioned by the removal of any part of the logs, was soon filled by others. The labor incident to the formation of a passage, through these small rafts, is so great, that the navigation of this part of the river is never attempted; for it would require to be repeated every time a passage was attempted.

On the morning of the 11th we reached a place, where a branch of the river, or a Bayou ran rapidly in from the north. Being informed by M. Touline (a French gentleman born in the Caddo Nation, and who now accompanied the party to that nation, to render his good offices) that it was absolutely impracticable to pass the great raft in boats of any kind; as neither Red nor White men had attempted it for 50 years before, and, that this was the only communication, through which the passage could be effected; we here left the river, and entered the Bayou.

The current in the Bayou is very rapid, it being the discharge for the water which runs out above the great raft: indeed, appearances seem to promise, that this will in time be the principal channel of the river, as no hope can be entertained of the great raft ever being removed.[52]

As the group finally left the Great Raft behind, they encountered an Indian runner who delivered the news that Spanish troops from Nacogdoches were marching to intercept them. The news was substantiated by Dr. Sibley, and the expedition feared the worst.[53]

On June 23rd, the group made an encampment near a

---

[52] Flores, Dan L.; Freeman, Thomas; and Custis, Peter. <u>Jefferson & Southwestern Exploration: The Freeman & Custis Accounts of the Red River Expedition of 1806.</u> Norman: University of Oklahoma Press, 1984.
[53] Cox, op.cit.

Coashutta Indian village. A second Indian messenger arrived to inform Freeman that the Spanish force that had been mustered against them now numbered three hundred strong. The Indian went on to say that the commander of the troops had entered a Caddo village near their camp and asked the chief if he loved Americans. The chief reportedly replied that he loved all men, and that the Spanish must not spill blood on Caddo land. The commander left without replying – a point that greatly troubled Freeman and his companions.[54]

The group remained camped there through July 11th, and they established relations with both the Coashutta and the Caddo. The Americans presented both tribes with flags, and documented many aspects of the natives' lives. During this period, however, the Indians continued to warn them against the Spanish.

Freeman, Custis, and crew finally continued their exploration upriver, and after two weeks they were met by three more runners from the Caddo, who told them an unsettling story. The Spanish commander, Don Francisco Viana, "a cross, bad man," had entered their village with several hundred troops. He saw the American flag that had been presented to the Indians when they visited the Freeman encampment, and he demanded that it be removed. When the Caddo did not immediately do so, he produced a knife and cut it down. The three braves begged the Americans to turn back and avoid a potentially violent conflict.[55]

Freeman was determined to press on, however, and follow President Jefferson's directive to "go forward until stopped by an overwhelming force."[56] By July 19th they had traveled another 125 miles, and the warnings continued. Since they were getting close to a possible encounter with the Spanish, the

---

[54] ibid.
[55] ibid.
[56] ibid.

Americans prepared a cache at an abandoned French military post where they could store part of their provisions and the field notes that had been taken so far.[57]

On July 28th, the sound of gunfire in the distance heralded the presence of Spanish. Two scouts were deployed to determine the position of the troops, and they returned the next morning to report that an encounter was eminent.[58]

The group proceeded cautiously, and while they were preparing their noon meal, a garrison of 150 Spanish soldiers on horseback and approximately fifty foot-soldiers entered their camp.

The Spanish commander, Captain Viana, informed the Americans that he was under orders not to let an armed force proceed into Spanish territory. Freeman responded that they were actually on American land, and were sent by the President on a mission of exploration. A stalemate ensued, with the Spanish commander holding firm to his position. Viana indicated that he would not waiver, and would let the officials from his government answer for his actions. He demanded to know when the Americans were going to go back.[59]

Being obviously outnumbered, and with Jefferson's directive to not engage in any direct military conflict with the Spaniards, Freeman had little choice. The waters of the river had been becoming more and more shallow due to the dry summer season, so it was evident that they could proceed only a short distance up the river anyway, so Freeman told the commander that they would start their journey back the next day.[60]

The Americans reached the Coashutta village by August 9th, and had returned to Natchitoches in another three weeks.

---

[57] ibid.
[58] Flores, op.cit.
[59] ibid.
[60] Cox, op.cit.

They brought back only a fraction of the information that some of their contemporaries who were on other explorations did, such as Lewis and Clark, and most regarded the entire affair to be a disappointment. It would be another thirteen years before the U.S. attempted another formal exploration of the same region.[61]

Map of the 1806 Red River Expedition. Published by Nicholas King in 1806. Courtesy of the United States Library of Congress Archives.

---

[61] ibid.

The Caddo Indians and the Raft

The first humans to be significantly affected by the Red River Raft were the natives that were indigenous to the area, the Caddo Indians. The Caddo lived in several tribal groups spread out through the four-state region comprised by southeast Oklahoma, southwest Arkansas, northwest Louisiana, and northeast Texas, from about 1000 A.D. to the early 1800s.[62]

They were a peaceful people, who relied on agriculture and hunting for sustenance. Crops such as corn, melons, squashes, and beans were common. Animals typical to their diet included deer, squirrel, birds, and fish.

The Caddo Indians that settled in the area of the Red River adapted to the marshy land, and dealt with the periodic flooding caused by the huge logjam.

One account by explorers who hired the Caddo as guides on the Red River mentions: "The Indian guides said that the Raft had always been there. Their oldest tribal stories mentioned it. Each year it grew upstream, the swamp creeping beside it. Where their ancestors had once had their largest village, Caddo Lake now ripples. This cursed barrier would always crawl on and on, devouring the river, ruining the country, and driving out the game. The gods themselves could

---

[62] Swanton, John R. Source Material on the History and Ethnology of the Caddo Indians. Norman: University of Oklahoma Press, 1996.

not stop it."[63]

In the journal of the Freeman-Custis Expedition, a prairie was described as extending on the eastern side of the Red River: "Beyond the prairie there is a large lake, on the west of which, and nearly thirty miles from Red River, lies the principal village of the Caddo. They reside on a small creek which empties into a lake that communicates with the river a little above the raft." (This lake that 'communicates with the river a little above the raft' would be today's Twelve Mile Bayou).[64]

Caddo Indians and Typical Dwellings,
U.S. Army Corps of Engineers Collection

The Great Raft kept the Caddo isolated, and unlike many tribes that had been forced off their land, the Caddo Indians enjoyed a peaceful coexistence with the settlers. In 1825, the United States signed a treaty with the Quapaw tribe living in Arkansas, and a move to Caddo territory was negotiated.

---

[63] Dorsey, Florence L. Master of the Mississippi: Henry Shreve and the Conquest of the Mississippi. New York: Houghton Mifflin Company, 1941.
[64] Gleason, Mildred S. Caddo: A Survey of Caddo Indians in Northeast Texas and Marion County 1541-1840. Jefferson: Marion County Historical Commission, 1981.

Article IV of the treaty states:

The Quapaw tribe of Indians will hereafter be concentrated and confined to the district of country in habited by the Caddo Indians, and form a part of said tribe. The said nation of Indians are to commence removing to the district allotted them before the twentieth day of January, eighteen hundred and twenty-six.[65]

The Caddo would not merge with the Quapaw, however, and gave them a very poor parcel of land that was located near the Red River Raft – land that the Caddo basically could not use and did not want. Constant flooding of the area was caused by the raft, and most of the Quapaw ended up going back to their original land, starving and in terrible condition.[66]

The Caddo Indians were allowed to stay on their lands and in 1830, Colonel Jehiel Brooks was appointed to be an agent of the United States Government to the natives.

On September 13th, 1836, Jehiel Brooks presented a Power of Attorney to the government that allowed him to conduct business for the Caddo, and the record of it was as follows:

I certify that Jehiel Brooks Esquire has deposited in this office a Power of Attorney from the "Chiefs, head men, and warriors of the Caddo Nation" which empowers him to receive from the Government of the United States all such amenities as shall from time to time become due to the Said Nation of Indians under the Treaty concluded with them on the 1st July 1835. – Second Auditors Office, September 13th 1836, O.S. Hall[67]

The Great Raft was causing water to flood the Caddo

---

[65] Glover, William B. "A History of the Caddo Indians." The Louisiana Historical Quarterly, Vol. 18, No. 4. October 1935.
[66] ibid.
[67] "Certificate of power of attorney from the Caddo Indians to Jehiel Brooks, September 13, 1836," The Brooks-Queen Family Collection, American Catholic History Research Center and University Archives, Catholic University of America, Washington, D.C.

lands, and some of the early, haphazard attempts to remove it only made matters worse. This was noted in a letter written on September 7th, 1832 that Brooks sent to the President after visiting the old site of the Caddo Prairie, and finding it flooded and in ruins:

On visiting the old site on the Caddo prairie, I found that it had been so often inundated that the grap, which clothed it like an artificial meadow, was supplanted by rank weeds. Every fruit tree and garden plant has perished in the floods; the foundations of buildings and lower floors, which had been frequently submerged, were rotten and crumbling in pieces. I also found that, instead of removing the obstructions out of the river, an attempt was making to turn it from its natural channel across this vary prairie, which would (so far as that object was practicable) increase the overflow on the prairie, by piling the water more rapidly upon lake Sodo, which is immediately below it. - Signed, J. Brooks, Indian Agent[68]

As efforts were begun to clear the Raft, the potential value of the land was realized, and the Indians were encouraged to sell the land and move to Indian Territory.[69]

On March 20th, 1834, Brooks wrote a letter to Judge E. Herring, the Commissioner of Indian Affairs, stating,

Since the practicability of removing the obstructions to the navigation of the Red River has been established, much excitement has been manifested respecting the river lands throughout the region of the raft, embracing a considerable scope of the Caddo territory, and is already a fruitful source of trouble to me and uneasiness to the nation. This state of things was anticipated by me from the first, and was the occasion of

---

[68] "Extracts from various letters relating to Jehiel Brooks' duties as an Indian Agent and Caddo Indians Lands, February 28, 1832 – August 19, 1835." The Brooks-Queen Family Collection, American Catholic History Research Center and University Archives, Catholic University of America, Washington, D.C.

[69] Glover, op.cit.

my suggesting to the President, when last in Washington, the necessity of extinguishing the Indian title to all such land prior to the removal of the raft.

As I have reason to believe that some branch of the Government has been addressed in regard to the lands, and as there are frequent attempts of late to encroach upon them, I have felt it my duty to apprise the register of land for this district of the occurrences, and now take leave to renew the suggestion, through you, whether it would not be best to negotiate for these lands at once, before the further progress of the work shall open the eyes of the tribe, as to their importance to the whites, or before their true interest shall be surrendered to the cupidity of the evil advisers who surrounded them.

I beg further to suggest that, if the Government approve of the above views, I believe the safest and best course of accomplishing the object will be between the Secretary of War and a delegation of the nation, at Washington City. By such a course of procedure, justice may be done between the parties without any of the embarrassments sure to at tend a negotiation here.[70]

Brooks wrote another letter to the Commissioner on July 1st, 1834, in which he said that the excitement over the eventual removal of the raft had brought land speculators in, some of which were actually – and illegally – making settlements on Caddo territory.[71]

This was one of the reasons that caused the Caddo to give up their land. Another was the fact that the U.S. continued to relocate other tribes of Indians onto Caddo lands. A third reason was that the Spanish encouraged them to move into Texas – land there had even been granted to them as an enticement.[72]

---

[70] ibid.

[71] ibid.

[72] ibid.

The Caddo finally realized that they could no longer hold onto their land. In March 1835, Brooks received instructions to negotiate with the Indians for the entire territory:

You will endeavor to procure a cession of their right to any land in that state. After considerable search and inquiry, I have not been able to ascertain, with precision, either the extent of the country occupied by them or the tenure by which it is held. The report of Colonel Many, a copy of which is enclosed, contains the best information in the possession of this Department on the subject. It appears probable, from this report, and from an examination of the map, that after the boundary line between the United States and Mexico is permanently established, the district of country occupied by these Indians may contain from six hundred thousand... to one million... acres. It is believed that the Caddo Indians are desirous of removing from the state of Louisiana, and their condition would be no doubt benefited by such removal.[73]

On June 3rd of that same year, Brooks contacted the interpreter for the Caddo Indians, Larkin Edwards, and asked him to visit the Caddo villages and inform the chiefs and people of the Caddo nation that he would be waiting at the Agency House on Peach Orchard Bluff to deal with them concerning the purchase of their land.[74]

On June 25th, the Caddo assembled – four hundred and eighty-nine, men, women, and children. They selected a council to represent them in negotiating the treaty of sale. On June 26th, the head chief, Tarshar, and underchief, Tsauninot, with twenty-three chosen councilors, met with Brooks at noon. They lighted the council pipe, and it was passed among those in attendance. Brooks proceeded to inform them that the President was pleased to hear that they had decided to sell their lands, and had appointed him to arrange the transaction. The

---

[73] ibid.
[74] ibid.

only points remaining were for Brooks and the council to reach an agreement on the price and conditions of payment. After the negotiation was finished, the Caddo would be required to vacate within a reasonable time.[75]

A Gathering of Caddo Indians, U.S. Army Corps of Engineers Collection

Brooks went on to say that that he was aware of the fact that many people had purported to be their friends and had advised them not to part with their lands, but he said, "I have never deceived you, and am again sent, as your friend, to obtain that from you which is of no manner of use to yourselves, and which the whites will soon deprive you of, right or wrong."[76]

When Brooks' statement was complete, Tsauninot, underchief of the Caddoes, addressed those assembled:

Brothers: We salute you, and through you, our great father, who has sent you again with words of comfort to us. We are in great want, and have been expecting you to bring us relief; for you told us, before you departed last fall, that you had no doubt our great father would treat with us for our

---

[75] ibid.
[76] ibid.

country, and would supply us with things of much more value to us than these lands, which yield no game. It is true that we have been advised by many not to make a treaty at all; that we would be cheated out of our land, and then driven away like dogs; and we have been promised a great deal if we refused to meet you in council. But we have placed no reliance on the advice and promises of these men, because we know what they want, and what they will do; and we have warned our people, from time to time, not to heed such tales, but wait and see what our great father would do for us. We now know his wishes, and believe he will deal justly with us. We will therefore go and consult together, and let you know tomorrow morning what we are willing to do.[77]

Brooks gave the Indians samples of the goods intended for them as part of the sale of the land. That afternoon he gave them more presents, this time telling them that the gifts were tokens of friendship, and that the items had nothing to do with the potential sale of the land. The council re-convened at ten o'clock in the morning, and Tsauninot informed Brooks that after the last meeting, his people had hung down their heads and were sorrowful.[78] Their head chief, Tarshar, rose and said:

My Children: For what do you mourn? Are you not starving in the midst of this land? And do you not travel far from it in quest of food? The game we live on is going farther off, and the white man is coming near to us; and is not our condition getting worse daily? Then why lament for the loss of that which yields us nothing but misery? Let us be wise then, and get all we can for it, and not wait till the white man steals it away, little by little, and then gives us nothing.[79]

When Tarshar had finished, the Caddo in attendance sprang to their feet with cries of satisfaction and gave their

---

[77] ibid.
[78] ibid.
[79] ibid.

The Caddo Indians and the Raft

support to selling their lands.

On July 1st, 1835, a new treaty was signed at the Indian Agency House on Peach Orchard Bluff. It sold the Caddo territory in northwest Louisiana to the United States for $80,000. Representing the Caddo nation was the Chief and twenty-four of his braves; Jehiel Brooks, the Indian Agent, represented the government. One parcel of land was reserved by the Caddo for Larkin Edwards, who had been their friend and interpreter. In addition, the Caddo agreed to "leave the United States forever, never to return." The ceremony was ended with a Corn Dance performed by the Caddo.[80]

The legal description of the land was as follows:

Bounded on the west by the north and south line which separates the United States from...Mexico, between the Sabine and Red River wheresoever the same shall be defined and acknowledged to be by the two governments. On the north and east by the Red river, from the point where the said north and south boundary line shall intersect the Red river whether it be in the territory of Arkansas or the State of Louisiana, following the meanders of the said river down to its junction with the Pascagoula Bayou. On the south by the said Pascagoula Bayou to its junction with Bayou Wallace, by said Bayou and Lake Wallace to the mouth of the Cypress Bayou thence up said bayou to the point of its intersection with the first mentioned north and south lines, following the meanders of the said water-courses; but if the said Cypress be not clearly definable, so far then from a point which shall be definable by a line due west, till it intersects the first mentioned north and south boundary line.[81]

By July 10th, the payment for the land – the goods and horses – had been delivered to the chiefs and head men of the

---

[80] Federal Writers' Project. <u>Louisiana: A Guide to the State</u>. New York: Hastings House, 1941.
[81] Glover, op.cit.

Caddo nation. Brooks reported that the Indians appeared to be well satisfied with the items received, and with the whole negotiation from the beginning to the end. The treaty was ratified by the United States Senate on January 26th, 1836, and then signed by President Andrew Jackson on February 2nd, 1836.[82]

There were some problems with the Caddo's adherence to the treaty, however. Many moved into Texas, but conflicts arose with the settlers there. It came to a head on November 21st, 1838, when the Adjutant General of the Republic of Texas wrote the Indian Agent in Shreveport to report, "the Caddo had spent their last installment of the $80,000 they had received from the sale of their lands to the United States on arms and ammunition, and that they were using these against the settlers in northern Texas."[83]

The conflicts escalated, and Texas troops under General Rusk entered Caddo Parish that same month. Yet another treaty was entered into a few days later on November 28th, 1838, in Shreveport. The Indians turned in their guns, and agreed to stay in Louisiana at the expense of the Republic of Texas until such a time when the Indian conflicts on the north side of Texas had been dealt with.[84]

Conflicts between settlers and various Indian tribes continued for several decades, however, although the Caddo remained peacefully neutral. An appeal was made to the U.S. Government in 1855 by Indian Agent Robert S. Neighbors on behalf of the Caddo, and a tract of land was allocated for them near the Brazos River. The tribe relocated there, and kept a very peaceful existence. They hunted, farmed, and even raised cattle on their new land. Aggressive tribes such as the Comanche continued to attack the settlers, and in 1859, the

---

[82] ibid.
[83] ibid.
[84] Federal Writers' Project. op.cit.

settlers decided to retaliate by launching a plan to massacre every reservation Indian regardless of their tribal affiliation.[85]

Agent Neighbors interceded on behalf of the Caddo, and put together a hastily organized march to new reservation land near the Washita River in Oklahoma. It was a grueling fifteen-day excursion in the summer heat of July, and the Caddo lost half of their livestock and other possessions in the process. For his trouble and concern, Neighbors was murdered by a settler, shot in the back by a man named Ed Cornett for his support and friendship of the Indians.[86]

The Caddo supported the Union in the Civil War, and were temporarily relocated to remove them from any areas of danger. Finally, in 1887 each tribal member was given land in Oklahoma and made an American citizen by decree of the Dawes Act.

By the turn of the twentieth century, the huge Caddo tribe – whose members had been the children of the Red River and had spent many generations adapting to life beside the Red River Raft – numbered only about five hundred individuals.

---

[85] Carter, op.cit.
[86] ibid.

The Shreve Years 1832-1841

In 1832, President Jackson could not ignore the problems brewing with the Indian Nations. The Red River would provide a clear passage into the region, so Jackson instructed his Secretary of War, Lewis Cass, to explore the possibilities of removing the Great Raft. The assignment was passed to Brigadier General Gratiot, the chief engineer. He, in turn, dispatched a young officer named Lieutenant W. Seawell to Louisiana for a first-hand look. After personally observing the Raft, Seawell concurred with Thomas Freeman's assessment from years before: removal of the Red River Raft was impossible.[87]

Upon hearing that report, Gratiot decided to call upon a man in whom he had gained great confidence over the years; a man who could clear the Raft if any human could: Captain Henry Shreve.

Henry Miller Shreve had been born to Isaiah and Mary Shreve on October 21st, 1785. He grew up in the area between the Youghiogheny and Monongahela rivers, and developed a love for river life. By the time that he was fourteen, he knew that his life would be spent on the water.

In the fall of 1807, at the age of twenty-two, Henry Shreve constructed a keelboat. He hired ten men for a crew and set off

---

[87] McCall, op.cit.

into the Monongahela River, headed for the Ohio River with a destination of St. Louis. Of his adventure, Shreve's Quaker father said, "It seems as if people are crazy to get afloat on the Ohio..."[88]

Captain Henry Miller Shreve

Reaching his destination in December, Shreve noted among the other strange things about the town that it boasted "a dozen billiard rooms and only one small church." He purchased a good many furs, traveled the river back home, carried them over the Allegheny Mountains, and finally arrived in Philadelphia where he sold them for a tidy profit.[89]

During other such excursions, while the crew of his ship busied themselves with drinking, gambling, and fighting during the idle hours, Shreve studied the meticulous notes that he had taken during his first river trip. He noted that the rivers of the Mississippi system could only be navigated for about half their lengths, "but their currents sorely hampered upstream going,

---

[88] Dorsey, Florence L. "Of Shreve & the River." Time Magazine. Monday, October 27, 1941.
[89] ibid.

and their piled and planted driftwood menaced craft on every side." Shreve didn't understand why these handicaps "were accepted with such inertia."[90] Given the right amount of capital, he felt that he could change the situation.

Shreve knew of the Sac and Fox Indians who had settlements on the Upper Mississippi River – he also knew that they mined and smelted lead. With a plan to bring him the wealth that he needed for his nautical aspirations, he took his keelboat and crew up the Mississippi. When he reached the rapids at Des Moines, "the crew went overboard, pulled the boat over eleven miles of successive ledges of stone, through boiling troughs, then through the eighteen miles of the upper rapids."[91]

The Sac and Fox Indians produced sixty tons of lead for him, and towing two additional boats, Shreve started the journey back down the Mississippi River. One account described the voyage as follows:

As the lead boats floated southward, the late July days were stifling...Bear and panther could break a path in the cane, and Indians crept in and out these trails...Heaped against the shore or rearing in the channel were dead drift-trees, overgrown with weeds and vines. Dully the alligators rose beside the driftwood, to view the boats and sink.

The slow-moving towboats passed Natchez with its women "as carefree as moths"; passed the great cane plantations; passed the seductions of New Orleans and the perils of the lower Delta. The piratical Brothers Lafitte did not molest Shreve's drab convoy, "never dreaming what a wealth of potential bullets lay in its hold." Shreve headed into the Gulf. By autumn he landed at Philadelphia, sold his lead for $11,000 profit. He had his capital – in cash, information, ideas. He stopped wearing Quaker clothes, bought himself a "worldly"

---

[90] ibid.
[91] ibid.

suit, got married.[92]

The year 1811 was one of a convergence of strange events. To begin with, the "Great Comet of 1811" streaked across the sky for approximately 260 days. It "was discovered on March 26th, 1811...it continued to increase in brightness during September, coming nearest to the earth on October 15th. By December it had become very faint. It could be seen in this country as well as in Europe."[93] The second event was a mass exodus of squirrels from the forest to the rivers, where many drowned themselves. In 1835, Charles Joseph Latrobe described the event:

Many things conspired to make the year 1811 the annus mirabilis of the West. During the earlier months, the waters of many of the great rivers overflowed their banks to a vast extent, and the whole country was in many parts covered from bluff to bluff. Unprecedented sickness followed. A spirit of change and recklessness seemed to pervade the very inhabitants of the forest. A countless multitude of squirrels, obeying some great and universal impulse, which none can know but the Spirit that gave them being, left their reckless and gamboling life, and their ancient places of retreat in the North, and were seen pressing forward by tens of thousands in a deep and solid phalanx to the South. No obstacles seemed to check their extraordinary and concerted movement. The word had been given them to go forth, and they obeyed it, though multitudes perished in the broad Ohio, which lay in their path.[94]

With a comet lighting up the night sky and thousands of lifeless squirrel bodies floating downstream, Shreve's boatmen were sure that it was all a cataclysmic sign. The final straw

---
[92] ibid.
[93] Halbert, H.S.; and Ball, T.H. The Creek War of 1813 and 1814. Chicago: Donohue & Henneberry, 1895.
[94] Latrobe, Charles Joseph. The Rambler in North America. London: R.B. Seeley & W. Burnside, 1835.

came when they observed Robert Fulton's steamboat chugging down the Mississippi. "Henry Shreve laughed at the superstitions of his boatmen, who believed the squirrels, the comet and the steamboat were portents of disaster. But in December a terrible earthquake tore the middle valley to pieces, sank dozens of flatboats and keelboats, smashed others on the bank. 'Shock followed shock, the ground rose and sank in sickening waves, the earth opened fissures a half-mile long, sulfurous gasses poured out...'"[95]

When Shreve learned that Fulton's steamboat the *New Orleans* had ridden out the tumultuous upheaval without incident, he immediately became fascinated with the concept of a ship powered by steam. As he watched Fulton's ship, however, he saw how much trouble that it had in shallow waters, and thought that one that had a much lesser draft would be more efficient.

Shreve's first experience with such a boat was one that was designed and built by Daniel French named the *Enterprise*. Henry Shreve sought after, and was subsequently named, captain of the ship. Although it was running between Brownsville and Louisville, Kentucky, he wanted to take the ship all the way down to New Orleans. Shreve departed Pittsburgh on December 21st, 1814 carrying a load of munitions for General Andrew Jackson to use in the defense of New Orleans against the British forces. They arrived, but because the Fulton-Livingston Company had established a monopoly on steamboats on the river, Shreve was met with legal resistance.[96]

He wanted to design his own ship, though, and while Fulton's *New Orleans* drew a deep draft in the river, Shreve envisioned a vessel that could pass through more shallow

---

[95] Dorsey, op.cit.
[96] Hunter, Louis C. <u>Steamboats on the Western Rivers: An Economic and Technological History.</u> Mineola: Courier Dover Publications, 1994.

The Shreve Years, 1832-1841

waters. He began construction on the new ship in Wheeling, West Virginia on the Ohio River. It was said that "talk of this hull never died...the vessel defied every principle of shipbuilding. It was exceedingly shallow of draft, but reared aloft with two decks, one above the other."[97]

Shreve launched his steamship, the *Washington*, in June 1816 bound for New Orleans. Before reaching his destination, however, a tragedy occurred at the town of Marietta, Ohio. The steamer had docked there for the evening, and when they set off the next morning a boiler exploded. The Captain and many of the crew and passengers were blown overboard into the river, injured by flying debris and the scalding steam and water. One account describes, "It was terrible beyond conception. Death and the most excruciating pain was spread around. Six or eight [people] were nearly skinned from head to feet, and others slightly scalded to the number of seventeen. In stripping off their clothes, the skin peeled with them."[98] Six died immediately, and seven soon thereafter. Saddened but undaunted, Shreve buried the dead, repaired the boiler, and set out once again. He finally steamed into New Orleans, intent on shattering the Fulton group's monopoly on the river.[99]

After surviving several legal battles with the Fulton-Livingston Company, Shreve emerged victorious – he had opened up the Mississippi to steam. In the two years that followed, sixty steamboats were built for the river.[100]

Having won that battle, Shreve then looked to a more formidable enemy – the river itself. The waterways were clogged with snags of trees and driftwood that made navigation perilous at best. Many companies, captains, and individual families lost everything when their craft hit such an

---

[97] Dorsey, op.cit.
[98] Hunter, op.cit.
[99] Kelman, Ari. A River and Its City: The Nature of Landscape in New Orleans. Berkeley: University of California Press, 2006.
[100] ibid.

impediment. It was a severe problem, and "for years, boat owners and settlers who had lost their craft or goods had pleaded with Congress to do something about the driftwood menace. The bewildered statesmen could offer no help. It was considered impossible to dislodge the enormous timbers: trees whose roots had dug deep into the stream bottom...were packed down with tons of silt..."[101]

Captain Henry M. Shreve Clearing the Great Raft from Red River, 1833-38,
by Lloyd Hawthorne (1924-2003),
courtesy of the R.W. Norton Art Gallery, Shreveport, La.

With his fame on the river, and desire to clear the rivers of timber snags, President John Quincy Adams appointed Shreve to the post of Superintendent of Western River Improvements in 1827.[102] A national reputation already existed for Adams'

---

[101] Dorsey, op.cit.
[102] Allen, Michael. <u>Western Rivermen, 1763-1861: Ohio and Mississippi Boatmen and the Myth of the Alligator Horse.</u> Baton Rouge: Louisiana State University Press, 1991.

choice: "the father of western steamboating, Henry Miller Shreve. At age forty-one this stout, bull-headed pilot was already larger than life. An outspoken Democrat, self-made and largely self-taught, Shreve was to steam navigation what Daniel Boone had been to the Kentucky frontier – its mythic hero, its symbol of raw genius..."[103]

Shreve accepted the position, and then set out to remove the snags with a boat capable of doing what none other could. He invented a steam-powered, "heavy-timbered, twin-hulled snag boat to do the job. He wrote the War Department, offering to submit a model. The War Department did not trouble to reply."[104]

The Snagboat Heliopolis, courtesy of the
U.S. Army Corps of Engineers Archives

---

[103] Shallat, Todd A. <u>Structures in the Stream: Water, Science, and the Rise of the U.S. Army Corps of Engineers.</u> Austin, University of Texas Press, 1994.
[104] Dorsey. op.cit.

Ever persistent, within a year Shreve's first snagboat, the *Heliopolis*, was under construction. When it was complete, the Captain finally got his chance to demonstrate his new boat. As one account explains: "While jeering onlookers hooted, the snag boat drove head on at a massive planter [a half-submerged tree]. There was a booming impact and crash. It seemed to the onlookers that the boat must be shattered to pieces. But there it was, still intact, and the huge tree toppling into the water. A spontaneous cheer went up."[105]

The snagboat proved to be invaluable on the river – "In going into action the snagboat was run full tilt at the projecting snag in such a manner as to catch it on the snag beam and force it up out of the water. This powerful blow was often enough either to break off the snag or to loosen it from the riverbed. Then the snag was brought under the snag beam, raised by the engine-powered machinery, and cut up. The heavy portions such as the stump and roots were either dropped into a deep pool or carried ashore for disposal while the remaining pieces were allowed to float harmlessly off. Snags weighing as much as seventy-five tons and embedded in the river for many feet were removed without difficulty by the snag boats, which were soon nicknamed *Uncle Sam's Toothpullers*."[106]

Soon progress was made toward clearing the snags on the Mississippi and Ohio Rivers, and stretches that even an experienced captain would never have traveled after dark could easily be traversed at night. The Red River, however, presented a different problem. The most phenomenal accumulation of snags in the other rivers were "minor obstructions" when compared to the Great Raft of the Red River. At that time, it began about twenty-five miles north of Natchitoches, and extended approximately one hundred and fifty miles up the

---

[105] ibid.
[106] Hunter, op.cit.

river.[107]

In 1832, Captain Shreve was ordered by Secretary of War Lewis Cass to attempt to remove the Great Raft on the Red River using his steam-powered boats. On April 11th, 1833, Captain Henry M. Shreve and the U.S. Army Corps of Engineers arrived at the lower end of the Raft, including 150 men and four snagboats.[108]

Two miles of the river was cleared of obstruction on the first day, and in four weeks some forty miles had been opened. When Shreve finally ended operations for the season in late June, a survey indicated that a full seventy-one miles had been cleared, almost half of the overall length of the raft.[109]

In 1835, eight businessmen headed by Angus McNeil formed the Shreve Town Company at the site of Captain Shreve's camp on the Red River. As the name implied, their purpose was to establish a city to be named Shreve Town; each partner was to contribute a proportionate share toward the purchase of land from Larkin Edwards and Francois Grappé, who had obtained it directly from the Caddo. Members of the company were McNeil, Col. James H. Cane, William S. Bennett, Bushrod Jenkins, Col. James B. Pickett, Sturges Sprague, Thomas T. Williamson, and Captain Henry Shreve. The city of Shreve Town was laid out in an eight-street by eight-street grid – the northernmost street was given the name Caddo in honor of the Indians from which the land had been purchased. The company began to sell lots in town, and they went quickly enough that the company members begin to see a profit in short order.[110]

Shreve became concerned that the United States agent to the Caddo Indians, Jehiel Brooks, had been misrepresenting the

---

[107] ibid.
[108] Wilkerson, Lyn. <u>Roads Less Traveled.</u> Bloomington: iUniverse, 2000.
[109] Hunter, op.cit.
[110] Carter, op.cit.

original selling of the land from the Caddo Indians to Grappé. He wrote a letter to President Jackson on April 29th, 1836, saying:

SIR: I have understood, from a source that can be relied upon, that an extensive fraud has been practiced on the United States by the agent of the Government making a treaty with the Caddo Indians in this vicinity in July last. Believing it to be my duty to give information in such cases, I relate the facts to you as I have them; they are as follows: The interpreter officiating in making the treaty was sworn to secrecy. This fact I have from the interpreter himself (John Edwards); a reserve was made of four leagues of land, commencing at the Pascagoula Bayou, running up the river for quantity, including all the land between the Bayou Pierre and Red River. By the meanders of the river, it will include a front of about thirty-six miles, and contain not less than 34,500 acres of the best lands on Red River...The reserve was made to a half-breed Caddo, or to his heirs, without any knowledge on their part of the transaction, until after the ratification of the treaty, when the agent came direct from Washington to Camplé, the resident of the half-breed's heirs, and bought from them the whole of the reserve at $6,000...I am also informed that the principal chiefs of the Caddoes did not understand that such a reserve had been made. The witnesses to the treaty were also ignorant of such a clause having been in it.[111]

Shreve's letter to the president had no effect, although it may have had some degree of merit, as witnessed by a document that was submitted to the U.S. Senate over a year later by twenty-one Caddo leaders, including Tarshar and Tsauninot, all of whom signed the document by making their "X" mark. The document reads:

They have, this 19th day of September, 1837, heard the treaty read and interpreted to them by a white man, who

---

[111] Carter, op.cit.

understands and speaks their language well...that they discover that the bounds and limits of the treaty are not such as they understood at the time of the treaty...that they, said chiefs, head men, and warriors, of the said Caddo Indians, never made any reserve to any person in the treaty aforesaid except to Mr. Larkin Edwards, an old white man that lived among them a long time; that Mr. Brooks, the Indian agent, told them that they could give Larkin Edwards a small piece of land if they wished to do so; that they then told Mr. Edwards that they would give him a small piece of land any where he wanted it in their lands. The said chiefs, head men, and warriors, would further represent unto your honorable body...that they never made any reserve to Francois Grappé, or any of his heirs or representatives, by the treaty, within the limits of land they claimed or sold to the United States.[112]

Several years later, the courts upheld Brook's title to the Grappé claim, and the land acquisition for the city of Shreve Town was deemed to have been legitimate.[113]

Any possible legal problems to the land did not stop the development of Shreve Town, however. When the first steamboat reached the city, the *Nick Biddle*, the future as a riverport became evident, and the name was changed to Shreveport.

The work on the Raft continued on, and Shreve was trying to reach the upper end by the time that work was halted for the summer of 1836, but he found the logjam to be denser than he had previously encountered. Many of his men fell prey to yellow fever, and work all but stopped. His report dated July 6th, 1836, claimed a loss of 9,006 man-days due to illness and attending to those who were sick. Twenty-one miles had been removed during work that season, with only nine miles of the Great Raft remaining. He gave the following description of it:

---

[112] ibid.
[113] Carter, op.cit.

"A deposit of mud had accumulated to such extent as to cover a large portion of the timber, on which the willow and cottonwood had sprung up and taken root on the logs of which the raft was composed. Many trees were found growing in that manner as large as eighteen inches in diameter."[114]

As soon as he stopped work on the Raft, it began to grow. Shreve and his crew began the clearing process once again in 1837. Just as they did, a Lt. A.H. Bowman arrived unexpectedly. Congress had dispatched him to the Red River to report on whether Captain was wasting the money that had been allocated for clearing the river. After much observation, Bowman submitted a report stating, "Shreve was doing a spectacular job under the most difficult of circumstances. Congress should not hesitate to approve funding; the money would be returned over and over again, in land sales, productivity, and reduced transportation costs."[115]

By the spring of 1838 the Red River had once again been opened as far north as the newly founded city of Shreveport, opening up trade for a total of three hundred miles. What had once been unsettled wilderness prone to flooding along the banks was now a continuous line of plantations.[116]

The work was completed that same year. Shreve's official report that year for the snag boats *Eradicator*, *Pearl* and *Laurel* read: "On March 1st, 1838, the first boat was enabled to force her way through the upper section of the raft, and up to [March] 29th five merchant steamboats passed up through the raft. On May 1st, the navigation through the extent of the raft was considered safe. There were two boats lost near the head of the raft – the *Black Hawk* and the *Revenue*. The amount expended in opening the raft has been $311,000."[117]

---

[114] McCall, op.cit.
[115] ibid.
[116] Louis, op.cit.
[117] Gould, op.cit.

The Shreve Years, 1832-1841

On September 12th, 1838, Shreve was granted patent number 913 for his snag boat that had so successfully been used to clear the river. It is not known why he waited so long to apply for the patent, when he could have obtained it years earlier.

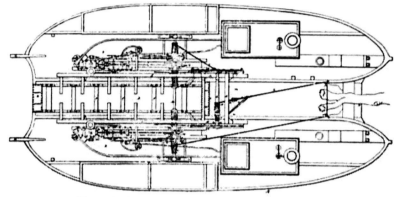

Shreve's Snag Boat Drawing From The Patent,
courtesy of the U.S. Library of Congress Archives

Shreve turned his attention to other duties as Superintendent. In June 1839, in his final report concerning the Great Raft, he noted that congressional action was necessary to keep the river clear and to prevent new buildup. Congress failed to act on his recommendation, however, and by 1841 steamboats again were blocked by snags on the Red River – the raft was re-forming.

In 1841, the political climate changed, and the Whig Party came into office. President John Tyler's administration relieved Shreve – who was a Jacksonian Democrat – of his position of Superintendent of Western River Improvements. At that time, he had a fleet of five snagboats, the fifth one named the *Henry M. Shreve*. The man that had been responsible for the initial clearing of the Great Raft drafted a letter to the War Department on September 11th, 1841, passing his job on to a successor.

The good Captain Shreve had completed his service on the Red River. He retired to his three-hundred-acre farm near St. Louis, where he applied to the government for compensation for inventing the snagboat that had proved to be so successful.[118]

The House of Representatives held a hearing on Shreve's claim, where Shreve stated:

Your petitioner respectfully represents, that he is the inventor of the steam snag-boats Heliopolis and Archimedes, the property of the United States, which are now and have been in the service of the government since 1829, under the direction of your petitioner as superintendent on the Mississippi and its waters. The invention has been attended with complete success; has answered all hopes of the inventor, and fully met the anticipations of the government.[119]

The House of Representatives denied him any compensation, summarizing it as follows:

It is incontestable that the government, in assenting to Shreve's building these boats, had no expectation that he would have or make a claim for the use of any invention made by him. He gave no notice that he intended to make such a claim, nor did he intimate anything of the kind. He furnished an estimate of their cost, but included nothing for the value of his invention. His must stop him from making any such claim, which would be neither legal nor equitable. He was bound to disclose all to the government, and if he had made an invention which he thought it ought to use he should have said so, and enabled it to determine for itself whether it would obtain the right to use it or not. By applying it on the government boats

---

[118] Hardin, J. Fair. "Henry Miller Shreve." Louisiana Historical Quarterly. Vol. 10, No. 1., January 1927.
[119] Reports From the Court of Claims Submitted to the House of Representatives During the First Session of the Thirty-Sixth Congress, 1859-1860. Washington: C. Wendell, 1860.

without giving any intimation that he was using for them a patentable invention of his own, he precludes himself from now insisting that it was wrongfully used, or that, in good conscience, he ought to be paid for it. He was not misled by the government, but, on the contrary, he now claims that he misled it. If the government now pays him what is demanded, the expense of the improvement will be increased beyond its expectations based on his estimates by the amount awarded to him. This would be unjust.

Whatever he could do in the furtherance of the enterprise in which the government was engaged, and the superintendence of which had been committed to him, he was bound to for the compensation he received.

Engineers in the army, architects in the navy, and officers in both, in the discharge of their duties, often display quite as much talent, ingenuity, and invention as Shreve did in this case, in contriving the means of annoyance and defense, and in the use of those means, without ever imagining that they had a right to charge the government for whatever they projected or did that had not been projected or done before.

Adopt the principle upon which this case rests, the army and navy would present and be entitled to endless reclamations. Men of ingenuity would not only be paid a high price for their services, because of that qualification, but they would ask to be paid ten times over, because they exercised it under their contracts as contemplated when they were employed. Such a principle, carried into practice, would soon bankrupt the government.[120]

Congress never appropriated compensation for Captain Shreve's invention of the snagboat. The public's opinion of the man, however is best summarized by the following statement: "To Captain Shreve the western people considered themselves most indebted, next to Fulton, for the early establishment of

---

[120] ibid.

steam navigation on their rivers, for having, in December of this year, on the first visit of the *Enterprise* to New Orleans, and subsequently with the *Washington* brought to a legal test, the claim of Fulton and his partners to a monopoly of the use of steam propulsion."[121]

Henry M. Shreve died in the home of his son-in-law, Walker Randolph Carter, on March 6th, 1851 and was buried in Bellefontaine Cemetery in St. Louis.

Henry Miller Shreve's Grave, courtesy of Bellefontaine Cemetery Archives

---

[121] Bishop, John Leander. <u>A History of American Manufacturers from 1608 to 1860.</u> Philadelphia: Edward Young & Company, 1866.

The Williamson Years 1842-1844

In 1841, with a portion of the raft already re-formed, Congress had no choice but to address the problem. An appropriation of $75,000 was made to remove the latest incarnation of the raft. Instead of placing the project under the Army Corps of Engineers, however, the job was let out to contract. The terms included the fact that the contractor would purchase the snag boat *Eradicator*, would then clear out the three miles of raft that had formed, and then keep the Red River clear for open navigation for a period of four years.[122]

Colonel Thomas Taylor Williamson, an original member of the Shreve Town Company, won the contract in 1842; he would resume the task of removing the Red River Raft. As a business associate of Captain Shreve, it was logically assumed that he would be a good candidate for the job. Williamson started by purchasing the snag boat *Eradicator* for $8,000.[123]

Confidence in Williamson was high, as witnessed by the following report by the *Daily Picayune* newspaper:

The Alexandria Whig states that there appears to be some hope, at last, that the raft of the Red River will be finally

---

[122] Abert, Colonel J J. November 15, 1844, 28th Cong., 2nd sess., Sen. Doc., vol. i, no. 1. Washington, 1844.
[123] Johnson, Leland R. The Falls City Engineers – A History of the Louisville District Corps of Engineers United States Army. Washington: U.S. Army Corps of Engineers, 1974.

removed, and the immense agricultural country above it be brought near to market by reason thereof. Messrs. Vawter and Williamson have made a contract with the government to the following effect, we understand. For the sum of $64,000 these gentlemen have contracted to remove the raft and keep the channel open for the space of five years. There can be but little doubt now that this work will be speedily accomplished, for the gentlemen engaged in it are thoroughly acquainted with the country, are acclimated and possess all the intelligence and active business habits in an undertaking of such magnitude. Mr. Williamson is already at the raft, busily at work and contemplates having it opened by the 1st of January, next. Laborers are in demand to work on it at $25 per month.[124]

    As it turned out, Williamson knew very little about the work that Shreve had done. Even with the snag boat *Eradicator*, he was unable to keep the river clear. In June of 1842 a freshet closed the Red River yet again; despite Williamson's efforts, rafts formed on the river that were greater than had been seen there before. The contractor had failed; he had accomplished little, if anything at all. In Williamson's defense, however, the flood of 1844 was one of the largest in recorded history. All the lands in the immediate neighborhood of Red River "were desolated, and every vestige of cultivation was destroyed." It is apparent that there was no way for Williamson to fulfill his obligations against such insurmountable odds.[125]

    Because of the lack of progress, however, on March 6th, 1844, Captain T.B. Linnard, the Superintendent who took Shreve's position, pronounced Williamson's contact with the government to be null and void.[126]

    Like many others before him, Capt. Linnard was

---

[124] "Removal of the Red River Raft." <u>Daily Picayune.</u> 18 November 1841.
[125] Abert. op.cit.
[126] ibid.

The Williamson Years, 1842-1844

convinced that removal of the Raft was impossible, largely because he believed that the riverbed had been raised by the presence of the Raft over the centuries. That led to his speculation that its flooding into adjoining streams and rivers could never be stopped, which would continue to feed fallen timber into the logjams. His proposed solution was to construct booms at specific places to force the river to cut new channels around the raft.[127]

The Army Corps of Engineers set out to implement his plan, but when the first book was constructed, it broke under the force of the water. By the spring of 1845 the Raft had become quite large, and Colonel Abert of the Army Corp of Engineers recommended that Shreve's brute-force techniques of removing the raft be resumed. When he approached Congress for appropriations for the work, he met with resistance.[128] Before approving any more funds, the Senate held an investigation of the Red River expenditures. During this time, the annexation of Texas to the U.S. and the outbreak of war with Mexico overshadowed the problems caused by the raft.[129]

With the government at a standstill, in 1846 an independent group of entrepreneurs attempted to set up a private system of transportation through the Raft. Traversing the series of logjams proved to be a fruitless exercise, so the endeavor failed.[130]

Once again, the Red River was closed to steamboats, and millions of dollars in trade were lost. Still, during the Mexican-American War that lasted from 1846 to 1848, and for several years afterward, operations on the Red River Raft were

---

[127] ibid.

[128] Abert, Colonel J.J. Report to Congress, November 1, 1845, 29th. Cong., 1st, sess., Sen. Doc., vol. iii, no. 26, pp. 5-13. Washington, 1845.

[129] ibid.

[130] Herbert, P.O. "The Red River Raft." Washington Telegraph. 18 March 1846.

suspended for lack of appropriations.[131]

When the war came to an end Congress was besieged with requests to clear the raft. The government's position was made clear by President Polk's message of March 13th, 1849, where he vetoed the internal improvement bill. Polk felt that the individual states should bear the expense of projects such as the clearing of the Raft, and that they should recoup their expenditures by taxing shipping and transportation on routes like the Red River.[132]

In spite of his failure at clearing the Red River, in 1851 Thomas T. Williamson received a majority vote for the DeSoto Parish representative to the State Legislature.[133]

Meanwhile, there was no work being done toward clearing the river – the Raft was left unchecked. Once again, it began to grow… the Red River Raft was rising from the ashes like a phoenix.

---

[131] ibid.
[132] 30th. Cong., 1st. sess., Ex. Doc., Vol. v, no. 49, pp. 1-17. Washington: 1849.
[133] DeSoto Parish, Louisiana 1850 Federal Census.

The Fuller Years 1850-1857

The next man to take on the arduous task of clearing the Red River Raft was Capt. Charles A. Fuller in the 1850s.

Fuller graduated from the United States Military Academy at West Point on July 1st, 1834, where he joined the army as a Bvt. Second Lieutenant in the 3rd Artillery. He was assigned to topographical duty – mapmaking – for a year, and after being promoted to First Lieutenant, fought in the Florida War against the Seminole Indians in 1835.[134]

Possibly it was the lure of a more lucrative civilian job, but for whatever reason, Lt. Fuller resigned the military on May 31st, 1837 and became a Civil Engineer in the service of the United States Government. He was appointed to be a U.S. Agent and Engineer for the Improvement of the Ohio River, where he served under Captain John Sanders in the Upper Ohio River project. Among other projects, Fuller was assigned to direct the construction of several dikes at various islands and shoals.[135]

He served until 1853, when he was tapped for service on the Red River.[136]

A survey was made of the Red River in 1854 to study the

---

[134] Cullum, Bvt. Maj.-Gen. George Washington. Biographical Register of the Officers and Graduates of the U.S. Military at West Point, N.Y., Vol. 1. New York: Houghton, Mifflin and Company, 1891.
[135] Johnson, op.cit.
[136] Cullum, op.cit.

area of the Raft and determine how to best deal with it. This report, which was submitted to Congress, indicated that the Red was blocked for thirteen miles at that time. The logjam was thick and heavy, however, and disposing of it would be no easy task. Fuller, serving as chief engineer on the project, favored diverting the river through lateral channels instead of attempting to clear the Raft, a task that he projected could cost as much as $12,000 per mile, which would require Congressional approval of over $150,000.00.[137]

Congress saw merit in this alternative plan, and finally gave their approval. Work began on the project in 1855 under Lt. Fuller, but progress was slowed because of an attack of cholera among the workers. At this point, the river had been completely blocked for two years by the Raft, and the large cotton crops in the upper region were being moved, albeit slowly, over land.[138]

Work on the re-routing plan continued through 1856. The proposed course was from Dooley's Bayou, to Soda Lake, and then Twelve Mile Bayou. By doing this, the hope was not only to shorten the course of the Red River, but also to increase its current.[139]

Very few maps exist of the steamboat routes during this period, because the government was focusing on circumventing the Red River Raft. The only map from the period, which shows a portion of the steamboat route between Shreveport, Louisiana and Jefferson, Texas, is by Fuller and was drawn in January 1855.[140]

---

[137] Red River Survey, 01/18-02/17/1855, 33rd Congress, 2nd Session, Sen. Ex. Doc., Vol. iii, No. 62. Washington: 1855.
[138] Fuller, Charles A. Annual Report to Congress, September 1, 1855, 34th Congress, 1st and 2nd Session, Sen. Doc., Vol. ii, No. 1. Washington: 1855.
[139] Red River Survey, op.cit.
[140] U.S. Army Corps of Engineers, Red River Waterway Project Shreveport, LA, to Daingerfield, TX, Reevaluation Study In-Progress Review. Washington: U.S. Army Corps of Engineers, 1992.

The Fuller Years, 1850-1857

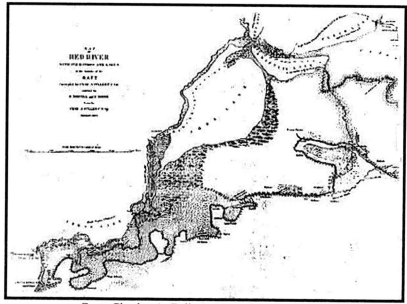

Capt. Charles A. Fuller's Map of the Red River

In 1856, an account of the Raft appeared in *DeBow's Review*, a magazine of "agricultural, commercial, and industrial progress and resource" that was widely distributed in the South during the mid- to late-1800s. It was named for its first editor, James Dunwoody Brownson DeBow, Professor of Political Economy, University of Louisiana. In the article DeBow gave his opinion regarding another article about the Red River Raft that appeared in a different magazine the previous year:

The Red River Raft Again – In the October Review, *1855, appears a very interesting and well written communication on the great Raft of Red River, which seems to me, on account if its great importance, deserves further notice. Your correspondent writes to show the great advantages resulting from the entire removal of the Raft; I, to show the probably, yes, very probably danger of its removal, and injury to lower part or all of Red River and N. Orleans. As certain as the same cause will produce the same effect, so certain will a new Raft* commence about or below Alexandria, when the present raft is removed. Your correspondent reasons well about the origin of the Raft, except a small error, which does not affect his main argument; this error was no doubt an oversight, or for the want of a little deeper thought, of which he was fully capable. He says the Raft was formed by the waters of the Mississippi being high from a freshet when Red river was low, its waters backed up and made still water at its mouth. The rafts of trees, logs, and drifts that came down the Red river was stopped by the ceasing of the current in this still water, and spread over the surface from bank to bank, and there accumulated. Your correspondent knows very well that there is no drift rafts or logs floating down the river when it is low. The raft, no doubt, was formed by the waters of the Red river during a flood running across from, below Alexandria, over a very low swamp, to Atchafalaya, when the Mississippi was high; backing up the water in Red river and forcing across the low lands as stated above. Still water then, as he states, was the cause of the beginning of the raft. His reasoning upon the age of the Raft, (400 years,) is very good; if it accumulates 1½ miles annually, and has ascended 600 miles, it is pretty clear that it has been about 400 years since it first begun. If the same cause will produce the same effect, as I have said, and all philosophers agree, why did not the Raft begin at an earlier date? This question may never be solved to the full satisfaction of people generally, but I will venture to give an opinion. Look upon a large map of North America, trace Red river to its junction with the Father of Waters, you will discover just below an outlet from the Mississippi about the same size in appearance of Red river, does it not look like the time may have been when Red river pursued its course down Atchafalaya to the Gulf, without being tributary to the great river? But the restless, mighty river, wallowing in its bed, broke through the banks of Red river and has since held its tributary. But it may be asked, what has this to do with it? My answer is, that the

The Fuller Years, 1850-1857

Mississippi runs on a ridge 12 or 15 feet above the common swamps, consequently when it first broke into Red river below, then the water of the Mississippi was forced back and across the lowlands below Alexandria, which would form an eddie or slack water between where the Red river waters escaped and the Mississippi. The drift of Red river not being able to follow its waters through the low timbered bottom to Atchafalaya, sloped with the first timber on the bank, and continued to increase until the Raft was formed, as your correspondent has stated. Now if the two rivers are as they were when the Raft was first formed, why would it not form again when both rivers are high? Twenty-five years ago I came up Red river on a steamboat, both river were high, there was then 25 or 30 miles of still or dead water between the mouth and first hills; I thought upon this subject, then came to the same conclusions as above, that if the Raft was removed it would of necessity begin again at its first beginning the very first high rise in both rivers at the same time. There is one remedy however that would prevent a new Raft forming below when the upper part should be removed, that is, make a levee from the high lands on the south side of the river to the mouth; this levee would force the water with a current sufficient to carry all the drift and logs to the Mississippi.

 I wrote a piece about two years since which was published in the Delta, wishing to call the attention of the engineers of the State of Louisiana to the subject, but they failed to notice it as far as I know. They may have discovered all my notions erroneous. But further, your correspondent tells of Caddo Lake, and he might have added all the other lakes on Red river were formed by the wearing of the banks of the Red river during the stay of the Raft at one point; this I believe is all correct, but they, though formed by the Raft, will remain lakes as long as time lasts; though the Raft rots away, the part of logs and drift that lie under water and mud, excluded from air, can never rot. There is no doubt, from the nature of things, a substratum of the Raft, some 8 or 10 feet thick, form the shoals at Alexandria to the head of the Raft. That the river bed is elevated to that height by the substratum. There may be a chain of rocks which form the shoals at Alexandria, as there seems to be chains over several rivers, and the shoals as Alexandria being in the line of this chain. But I would not be astonished to yet learn that the shoals are formed by logs on the foot of the Raft; at least if there had been no rocks there, there would necessarily be a shoal at the foot of the substratum of the original Raft.[141]

By 1857, there was a concern about the rapids at Alexandria, and it was feared that the new plan would only increase this problem.[142] The attempt to re-direct the river was abandoned in favor of another assault directly on the Great Raft. In the next few years, support for any efforts on the Red River began to wane, however, in the wake of the domestic difficulties that preceded the upcoming War Between the States.[143] With the appropriation funds exhausted with little accomplishment toward the goal of clearing the Raft, the work was abandoned.[144]

Speculation does exist that Fuller's efforts were not in accordance with the standing orders regarding the Red River at that time, as indicated by this passage from *Biographical and Historical Memoirs of Northwest Louisiana*:

Instead of cutting the twelve miles of raft between Carolina Bluffs and Gilmer, he [Fuller] *contented himself with cutting canals at the head and foot of Dutch John's Lake and to*

---

[141] DeBow, J.D.B., "Red River Raft Again." Debow's Review Vol. XXI. – Third Series, Vol. I. 1856.

[142] Abert, Colonel J.J., Report to Secretary Davis, 03/15/1856, 34th Congress, 1st Session, Sen. Ex. Doc., Vol. xii, No. 49. Washington: 1856.

[143] Abert, Colonel J.J., Report to Congress, November 14, 1860, 36th Congress, Sen. Doc., Vol. ii, No. 1. Washington: 1860.

[144] Northrop, E.B.; Chittenden, H.A.; and Bishop, W.H. "The Red River Raft." The Wisconsin Lumberman. 1873.

sundry work on Dooley's Bayou, with the object of throwing the water into Soto Lake [a.k.a. Soda Lake]. This useless work cost the United States $90,000. The plans on which Fuller acted were said to be inspired by James B. Gilmer, who at this time was hostile to Shreveport[145].

Gilmer was a landowner in the region who may have feared that his interests would be harmed by the removal of the Raft, and therefore exerted influence on Miller.[146]

Whatever the case, without government efforts to clear the Raft, it would most likely begin to re-build, so in 1859 interested parties from the three concerned states gathered in Shreveport for the purpose of forming a company to be named "The Louisiana, Arkansas, and Texas Navigation Company." Delegates in attendance were N.D. Ellis representing Texas, Col. C.M. Hervey representing Arkansas, and Dr. T.P. Hotchkiss and John M. Landrum representing Louisiana. The company was to be funded with an initial stock offering to raise $250,000.00, which they hoped would be provided by plantation owners all along the river. The investment would be recouped by a toll that would be charged on the freight-bearing vessels that traveled up and down the Red.

Apparently the company was to be formed out of frustration with the amount of money that the U.S. Government had already wasted on the project. One account explains:

This accumulation of drift has been a fruitful speculation for more parties than one – appropriations have been wasted on it, sufficient, if judiciously expended, to have removed and kept free from impediment, every foot of the river from its confluence with the Mississippi to the mouth of the Kianeche; and though this raft has baffled the exertions of government,

---

[145] Southern Publishing Company. <u>Biographical and Historical Memoirs of Northwest Louisiana.</u> Chicago: Southern Publishing Company, 1890.
[146] O'Pry, Maude Hearn. <u>Chronicles of Shreveport and Caddo Parish.</u> Shreveport: Journal Print Company, 1928.

agents and employes [SIC], *it will, before the well-organized and properly well-directed efforts of the gentlemen who are now moving in the matter, disappear like frost before the sun.*[147]

The company progressed no further than the paper stage of the project. Congress was still considering granting consent for the company's plan when the Civil War broke out, which effectively ended any further action. Remaining unchecked, again, the Raft began to slowly grow.[148]

The Great Red River Raft, courtesy of the
LSU-Shreveport Archives, Noel Memorial Library

---

[147] DeBow, J.D.B. "Red River Raft." Debow's Review Vol. XXVI. – Third Series, Vol. I. 1859.
[148] Humphreys, Hubert Davis. "The 'Great Raft' of the Red River." North Louisiana, Volume One: To 1865, Essays on the Region and Its History. Ruston: McGinty Trust Fund Publications, 1984.

The Civil War and The Raft
1861-1865

During the Civil War years, the Red River Raft was left untouched, since the Confederacy did not have the time, money, or resources to enhance their transportation and commerce infrastructure. In fact, the Confederate Constitution forbade such improvements:

The Congress shall have power... to regulate commerce with foreign nations, and among the several States, and with the Indian tribes; but neither this, nor any other clause contained in the Constitution, shall ever be construed to delegate the power to Congress to appropriate money for any internal improvement intended to facilitate commerce; except for the purpose of furnishing lights, beacons, and buoys, and other aids to navigation upon the coasts, and the improvement of harbors and the removing of obstructions in river navigation; in all which cases such duties shall be laid on the navigation facilitated thereby as may be necessary to pay the costs and expenses thereof.[149]

Although there was no work toward clearing the Raft during the Civil War years, an impressive feat of engineering

---

[149] Constitution of the Confederate States of America, as adopted on March 11, 1861, Article 1, Section 8, Paragraph 3.

occurred on the Red River as part of what is now known as the "Red River Campaign."

In 1864, President Lincoln began to consider the importance of taking the Red River. There were rumblings that a combination of French and Mexican forces might join with the Confederacy against the Union, streaming across the Rio Grande to shore up the struggling Southern forces. Riverports such as Shreveport, Louisiana and Jefferson, Texas were being used as lifelines of support to the Southern troops. Even more importantly, the New England mills were running out of cotton, and they desperately needed more raw material. These problems would all be solved if the Union could achieve one specific goal: seizing the cotton plantations along the Red River in Louisiana, and then finally, taking Texas.

The Red River was the obvious choice for the approach, and an assault was planned with 36,000 troops under the command of Union General N.P. Banks, supported by a fifty-eight-ship flotilla, including 13 ironclad ships and seven light-draught gunboats of the navy under Admiral D.D. Porter.

The Red River Campaign started on March 10th, 1864, when the Union Naval forces began to make their way up the Red River. General Banks marched his troops along with them, following a river road. It was a formidable force indeed, and one that could have well accomplished their mission, had it not been for a blunder on the part of the Army of the North: Banks eventually separated his land forces from Porter's naval fleet. The plan was to rendezvous in Shreveport, but that never came to pass.

Porter's forces would be hopelessly blocked between Shreveport and Natchitoches. Admiral Porter described what the Union Navy encountered:

When I arrived at Springfield Landing I found a sight that made me laugh. It was the smartest thing I ever knew the rebels to do. They had gotten that huge steamer New Falls City *across Red River, one mile above Loggy Bayou, fifteen feet of*

The Civil War and the Raft, 1861-1865

her on shore on each side, the boat broken down in the middle, and a sand bar making below her. An invitation in large letters to attend a ball in Shreveport was kindly left stuck up by the rebels, which invitation we were never able to accept."[150]

Steamship *New Falls City,* courtesy of
The Public Library of Cincinnati and Hamilton County

While Porter and his men were contemplating how to remove the obstruction, word reached them of the defeat of Banks' land forces at Mansfield and Pleasant Hill, and their hasty retreat. The Naval vessels were ordered to turn around and return south to rendezvous with the ground troops.

As they proceeded along the Red River, the water levels began to fall, giving Porter great concern that the ships would be grounded before they passed the Alexandria rapids. The decline in the water's depth was a direct result of Confederate actions to impede the Union Navy. The grounding of the *New Falls City* provided a makeshift dam that started the process.

---

[150] Louisiana Naval War Commission. "Louisiana's Military Heritage: Battles, Campaigns, and Maneuvers." 2006.
<http://www.usskidd.com/battles-redriver.html>

Next, southern engineers blew up an established dam, which diverted the river into Bayou Pierre, which dropped the water level significantly.[151]

Admiral Porter's fleet on the Red River, courtesy of Library of Congress

By the time that Porter's boats neared Alexandria, the river had become too shallow for passage – only three feet, four inches. The Admiral was faced with the choice of abandoning the vessels, in effect giving the Confederates two million dollars worth of naval equipment, or burning them to keep them out of enemy hands.[152]

Lieutenant Colonel Joseph Bailey of the Corps of Engineers proposed the building of a crib-and-tree dam, similar to ones that he had previously built in Wisconsin and at Port Hudson. His plan was met with apprehension, and in fact, Porter joked with him saying, "If you can dam better than I

---

[151] Tucker, Spencer. Blue & Gray Navies: The Civil War Afloat. Annapolis: Naval Institute Press, 2006.
[152] ibid.

can, you must be a good hand at it, for I have been damning all night!"[153]

Desperate times require desperate measures, however, and Bailey was given permission to start. Porter dispatched a messenger, saying, "Tell General Franklin that if he [Bailey] will build a dam or anything else, and get me out of this scrape, I'll be eternally grateful to him."[154]

Bailey started construction on both sides of the river, using a different technique on either side. On the west bank, he constructed large boxes, or cribs, that were placed end-to-end out into the river. Any available lumber was used – homes, barns, and businesses were stripped of their siding. When each box was put into the river, it was filled with stone or brick to give it weight, and therefore strength against the current. On the east bank there was a lack of cut lumber, so trees from the forest were felled and stacked lengthwise with the current, and anchored to the bottom with rocks.[155]

Of the construction, Porter would later write, "The proposition looked like madness, and the best engineers ridiculed it, but Colonel Bailey was so sanguine of success that I requested General Banks to have it done, and he entered heartily in the work."[156]

The makeshift dams on either side did not quite meet in the middle, so barges were used to fill the gaps. Bailey's plan worked – the water began to rise. When it was at a level to allow the draft needed by the boats, the water broke through one of the barges and created an opening. The Union vessels rode the wave of water to safety.

---

[153] Hoffman, Wickham. Camp Court and Seige. New York: Harper & Brothers, 1877.
[154] ibid.
[155] Smith, Steven D.; and Castille, George J. III. Bailey's Dam. Baton Rouge: Louisiana Archeological Survey and Antiquities Commission, 1986.
[156] Beecher, Harris H. Record of the 114th Regiment N. YS. V. Norwich: J.F. Hubbard, Jr., 1866.

Bailey was the man of the hour. He was presented with a silver sword and Tiffany's punchbowl by the naval offers, and Congress confirmed his promotion to Brigadier General. In the press of the day he was declared *Hero of the Red River*.[157] With Bailey's obvious engineering prowess, one has to wonder what he could have accomplished if he had been assigned to the task of clearing the Red River Raft.

Bailey's Dam under construction May 1865,
courtesy of the National Archives

When the Civil War ended, the country busied itself with the task known as "reconstruction," and the war-weakened government had no resources to commit to the clearing of the Great Raft, although citizens of the region were still very interested in the project. A convention was held in 1869 in the city of New Orleans to discuss the clearing of the Raft, but the widely varied opinions of the delegates made the endeavor end

---

[157] Goc, Michael J. Hero of the Red River, The Life and Times of Joseph Bailey. Friendship: New Past Press, 2007.

in failure.[158]

It would be another year before the government would once again take interest in clearing the Great Raft.

A cleared area, with more of the Raft in the distance, courtesy of the LSU-Shreveport Archives, Noel Memorial Library

---

[158] Caldwell, Norman W. "The Red River Raft." <u>Chronicles of Oklahoma,</u> <u>Vol. 19, No. 3.</u> September 1941.

The Final Taming of the Raft 1871-1873

The United States Government again began to consider the clearing of the Raft in the early 1870s, when it called for a survey of the Red River in the River and Harbor Act of March 3rd, 1871.[159]

Lieutenant E.A. Woodruff of the Corps of Engineers made the survey in 1872, and reported that, "The total length of the raft covering the whole breadth of the river is seven miles, but throughout almost all of the distance between the head and foot of the raft the channel is partially obstructed. The whole area of floating raft is computed at 290 acres. The whole area of 'tow-heads' or raft resting on bottom… is computed at 103 acres."[160] Woodruff submitted a plan for removing the raft, which was accepted by Congress.

An appropriation of $150,000.00 was made – the removal of the Raft would be attempted once again. Captain C.W. Howell of the New Orleans District Corps of Engineers was placed in charge of the endeavor, and he directed Lt. Eugene Augustus Woodruff to take the snag boat *Aid*, three crane boats, and a transport boat, and begin the operation. Although

---

[159] Bagur, op.cit.
[160] Woodruff, A.E. Report of the Chief of Engineers, October 19, 1872, 42nd Congress, 3rd SessionEx. Doc. No.1, pt. 2, vol. ii, p. 61. Washington: U.S. Army Corps of Engineers, 1872.

The Final Taming of the Raft, 1871-1873

the length of the Raft was not expansive, it would be quite an undertaking. The logs and mud had formed a solid mass, and at places there were "groves of trees a foot thick" growing on top of it, as if it were land.[161]

A similar description was published in the *Wisconsin Lumberman*: "Logs, roots and snags of every description had been crowded and jammed into a tangled mass, becoming more compact each year as the pressure from above increased. Annual freshets had brought down mud and deposited it in and over this mass until, in places, the raft itself had become entirely covered with earth, small islands or 'tow-heads,' thus being formed. Upon these tow-heads were growing trees, usually willows, three feet and more in circumference."[162]

Woodruff used not only the snag boats invented by Capt. Shreve, but also brought in saw boats and crane boats to help with the task. When all else failed, nitroglycerin was used to break apart the Raft. One of Woodruff's assistants wrote, "Nitroglycerine is the effective agent in opening jams, and is carried constantly on the *Kalbaugh* for this purpose. No fears are entertained by either the captain or crew in its use, and it is considered indispensable in keeping the river open during present stage of water."[163]

Cans that contained ten to twenty pounds of the explosive would be sunk as near to the bottom of the river as possible, and then ignited.[164]

The *New York Times*, August 30th, 1873, wrote about the progress on the Raft:

A New Orleans paper gives an extended account of the work being done in destroying the immense accumulation of

---

[161] O'Pry, op.cit.
[162] Northrop, op.cit.
[163] U.S. War Department. Annual Report of the Secretary of War. Washington: U.S. Govt. Printing Office, 1874.
[164] Guthrie, Keith. Texas Forgotten Ports, Vol. II. Austin: Eakin Press, 1993.

drift-wood in the Red River, which has for years past checked all navigation there. The work is done under the supervision of Lieut. Woodruff, and the expenses defrayed by the National Government. Up to this time a channel sufficient for the purposes of navigation has been opened through four miles of a raft – that is, actual raft – but comprising a much larger distance of actual outline of river. The saving is in enabling vessels to avoid the dangerous route through Black Bayou. The whole obstruction originally comprised about seven miles of raft; there therefore remains about three or three and a half miles yet to be cleaned out. It is thought this will prove comparatively easy, although possibly requiring longer time on account of the greater bulk of the upper raft and the greater breadth of the river. Lieut. Woodruff estimates that his work will be accomplished by the first day of November next. At the last session of Congress a second appropriation of $80,000 was made, and it is believed this will prove ample to complete the work; but Congress may adopt the views of Major Howell, and make an additional appropriation for the destruction of all accumulations of drift-wood and trees growing near the river for several hundreds of miles beyond the present scene of operations. A new cotton region will be opened and utilized by the removal of the raft. The lands above it have hitherto been comparatively valueless. They will be reclaimed. Above and beyond the raft spreads out a royal country, whose power of production will soon be seen and felt in the cargoes of cotton it will send to New Orleans.[165]

 The *New York Times* article was published on August 30th, and although Woodruff was optimistically quoted therein, tragedy was just around the bend. He arrived in Shreveport that very same day aboard the ship *Sterling* to obtain supplies, and discovered the city was in the throws of a yellow fever

---

[165] "The Removal of the Red River Raft". <u>The New York Times</u>. 30 August 1873.

epidemic. He decided to stay for a while and help with the disastrous effect the disease was having on the city. He joined the Howard Association, a volunteer organization to fight yellow fever, on September 4th, and was assigned to patrol the streets to identify those infected with yellow fever, and to keep order in the city. On September 15th, 1873, however, Woodruff contracted the deadly disease himself. He was taken to a hospital bed, and died only two weeks later on September 30th... "a martyr," reported a local newspaper, "to the blessed cause of charity." He never saw his dream of clearing the Red River Raft come true.[166]

Eugene Woodruff's grave in Shreveport, LA

Captain Howell wrote the following tribute to Eugene Woodruff: "He died because he was too brave to abandon his post even in the face of a fearful pestilence and too humane to let his fellow beings perish without giving all the aid in his

---

[166] Army Corps of Engineers, Tulsa District. "Flash from the Past." Tulsa District Record. March/April 2001.

power to save them. His name should be cherished, not only by his many personal friends, but by the Army, as one who lived purely, labored faithfully, and died in the path of duty."[167]

Woodruff was buried in Oakland Cemetery in Shreveport.

Upon Eugene's death, his brother George Woodruff was named as the successor. Since he was the personal confidant of his brother, he was already well versed in the project, and could ensure that no interruption of work occurred.[168]

George saw the raft removal project to its completion in December of 1873. In the next year, George gave tribute to his brother by christening a new U.S. snag boat the *E.A. Woodruff*, which served on the Ohio River until 1925.[169]

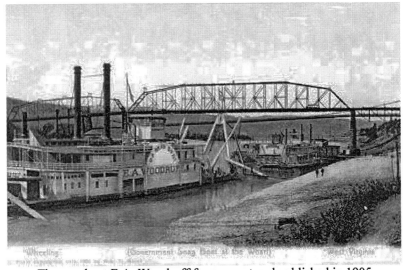

The snagboat E.A. Woodruff from a postcard published in 1905

Back in 1806, the explorer and adventurer Thomas Freeman had gazed upon the mammoth logjam and stated that

---

[167] ibid.
[168] United States War Department, op.cit.
[169] Army Corps of Engineers, op.cit.

The Final Taming of the Raft, 1871-1873

there was no hope of the Great Raft ever being removed. After almost seventy years of trying to tame the beast, however, and the efforts of many men, the task had finally, and forevermore, been achieved.

Today, the Red flows freely where the Great Raft once impeded all river traffic.

The Red River today, clear and open

Timeline of the Red River Raft

1719 – Explorer Bernard de La Harpe encountered the Great Red River Raft.

1722 – Raft is shown on a map by cartographer J.F. Broutin on his *Carte des Natchitoches*, or "map of Natchitoches."

1763 – Spain receives Louisiana from France as part of the Treaty of Paris.

1800 – Spain cedes Louisiana back to France in the Treaty of San Ildefonso.

1803 – The Louisiana Purchase is made from France by the United States.

1804 – Dunbar-Hunter Expedition is launched to explore the Red River watershed.

1805 – Dr. John Sibley records that the raft extends as far south as Campti.

1806 – Freeman and Custis Expedition encounters the Great Raft, and says, "No hope can be entertained of the great raft ever being removed."

Timeline of the Red River Raft

1811 – First of New Madrid, Missouri earthquakes shake the United States.

1812 – Louisiana granted statehood.

1814 – Henry Miller Shreve secures the position as Captain of the steamship *Enterprise*.

1815 – Captain Shreve first sees the Great Raft.

1816 – Shreve launches the steamship *Washington* bound for New Orleans, and has the first steamship explosion.

1824 – U.S. War Department orders a survey of the raft region.

1825 – Arkansas Territorial Legislature petitions Congress to remove the raft.

1826 – Army Engineers from Fort Jesup spend two months examining the raft.

1826 – Congress appropriates $25,000 to begin work on removing the Raft.

1827 – Captain Shreve assumes the post of "Superintendent of Western River Improvement."

1828 – Dr. Joseph Paxton submits arguments to Congress on removing the Raft.

1828 – Captain Shreve invents and builds the first steam-powered snagboat, the *Heliopolis*.

1829 – Army work on removing the raft began.

1830 – Army work was stopped, when Congress approved no more funds.

1832 – Congress appropriates $20,000 for work on the raft

1832 – Captain Shreve of the Army Corps of Engineers is ordered to begin removing the Great Raft.

1833 – Preliminary government survey determined the Raft to be 128 miles long.

1833 – Captain Shreve arrives at the foot of the Raft to begin work.

1833 – Congress failed to approve more money, and so work stopped.

1834 – Money is finally approved, and work is started again.

1834 – LA Governor Alexander Mouton sold all state-owned steamboats, equipment and slaves used to remove the raft.

1835 – Caddo Indians sign a treaty to sell all of their land at the upper part of the Red River to the United States.

1835 – The Shreve Town Company is formed by eight businessmen.

1836 – Only nine miles of the raft remain, but these are much more dense than had previously been encountered.

1836 – Ships were going as far north as Coates's Bluff, some 110 miles above the original foot of the raft.

Timeline of the Red River Raft

1836 – City of Shreveport Incorporated

1838 – Shreve is granted a U.S. Patent on his snagboat.

1838 – Shreve announced that he had cleared a passage completely through the raft.

1838 – By August, several places in the raft had become clogged with logs once again.

1838 – Shreve asked for (and received) more money, but he failed to keep the river open.

1839 – Private funding of $7147.50 allowed Shreve to open a passage once again.

1840 – Bill passes senate to appropriate funds to remove the raft.

1841 - $425,800 had been spent by the government to date on the raft removal project.

1841 – Capt. Shreve relieved of the office of "Superintendent of Western Rivers Improvement" by the new Whig administration – he retires.

1841 – Col. Thomas T. Williamson makes a contract with the government to remove raft.

1842 – Thomas Taylor Williamson begin work on the raft

1844 – The worst flood in the Red River area in recorded history occurs, making any progress toward clearing the Raft impossible.

No Hope! The Story of the Great Red River Raft

1844 – Failing to clear the raft, Williamson's contact was declared to be void.

1846 – The Mexican-American War breaks out, and all excess funding is directed toward it; no money exists for work on the Raft.

1849 – President James Polk took office and refuses all proposed expenditures on clearing the Red River.

1850 – A new congressional Appropriation of $100,000 is made to clear the Raft.

1850 – Capt. Charles A. Fuller, U.S.B.C. begin clearing raft.

1851 – Captain Shreve dies and is buried in St Louis.

1854 – A new survey was made, and the Red River was found to be obstructed for a total of thirteen miles.

1854 – Congress approved new funds to clear the raft.

1855 – Fuller files a report to Congress, dated Sept 1, 1855, saying that the river had been completely closed for two years and the large cotton crops in the upper region of the Red River could not be moved, except over land. He proposes redirecting the river instead of clearing it.

1857 – The idea of diversion is abandoned, and Capt. Fuller ended his work on the raft.

1864 – The Red River Campaign was launched against Shreveport, but the Union ships could not make it up the river.

Timeline of the Red River Raft

1869 – A convention was held in New Orleans to discuss the improvement of navigation on the Red River, but no progress was made.

1870 – The River & Harbor Act of March 3, 1871 calls for a new survey of the Red River. It is determined that seven miles of the raft exist at that time, covering some 290 acres of the river.

1872 – Federal Government appropriates $170,000 for work on the Red River.

1872 – Lt. Eugene August Woodruff, leader of the Army Corps of Engineers, was place in charge of removing the raft under Captain C.W. Howell.

1873 – Navigable channel completed.

1873 – Steamboat R. T. Bryarly passed through the length of the raft.

1873 – Congress appropriated funds for permanent removal of the raft.

1873 – Lt. Eugene A. Woodruff begins removing the raft using craneboats, dynamite, and tri-nitroglycerin.

1873 – Woodruff leaves his troops to visit Shreveport and recruit a surveying party. He dies from a yellow fever epidemic there.

1873 – George Woodruff, Eugene's brother, completes removal of the raft.

1874 – Red River became partially closed by driftwood again.

1876 – Engineers announced plans for a channel 150 feet in width to be cut through the raft.

1878 – Appropriations were made to for more work on the raft area.

1880 – The raft had been tamed, but to keep it as such required constant patrolling and clearing of the river.

1892 – Congress authorizes the Red River below Fulton, Arkansas Project.

Bibliography – Books Cited

Allen, John Logan. <u>North American Exploration: A Continent Comprehended.</u> Lincoln: University of Nebraska Press, 1997.

Allen, Michael. <u>Western Rivermen, 1763-1861: Ohio and Mississippi Boatmen and the Myth of the Alligator Horse.</u> Baton Rouge: Louisiana State University Press, 1991.

Bagur, Jacques D. <u>A History of Navigation on Cypress Bayou and the Lakes.</u> Denton: University of North Texas Press, 2001.

Beecher, Harris H. <u>Record of the 114th Regiment N. YS. V.</u> Norwich: J.F. Hubbard, Jr., 1866.

Bishop, John Leander. <u>A History of American Manufacturers from 1608 to 1860.</u> Philadelphia: Edward Young & Company, 1866.

Carter, Cecile Elkins. <u>Caddo Indians: Where We Come From.</u> Norman: University of Oklahoma Press, 2001.

Cullum, Bvt. Maj.-Gen. George Washington. <u>Biographical Register of the Officers and Graduates of the U.S. Military at West Point, N.Y., Vol. 1.</u> New York: Houghton, Mifflin and Company, 1891.

Dennedy, David M.; Cohen, Lizabeth; and Bailey, Thomas A. <u>The American Pageant.</u> Florence: Wadsworth Publishing, 2001.

Dewees, W.B. Letters From an Early Settler of Texas. Louisville: Hull & Brothers, 1854.

Dorsey, Florence L. Master of the Mississippi: Henry Shreve and the Conquest of the Mississippi. New York: Houghton Mifflin Company, 1941.

Dunbar, William. Journal of a Voyage... to the Mouth of the Red River. Philadelphia: American Philosophical Society, 1809.

Dunbar, William; Hunter, George; Berry, Trey; Beasley, Pam; and Clements, Jeanne. The Forgotten Expedition, 1804-1805. Baton Rouge: Louisiana State University Press, 2006.

Federal Writers' Project. Louisiana: A Guide to the State. New York: Hastings House, 1941.

Feldman, Jay. When the Mississippi Ran Backwards. New York: Simon and Schuster, 2005.

Fletcher, John Gould. Arkansas. Fayetteville: University of Arkansas Press, 1995.

Flores, Dan L.; Freeman, Thomas; and Custis, Peter. Jefferson & Southwestern Exploration: The Freeman & Custis Accounts of the Red River Expedition of 1806. Norman: University of Oklahoma Press, 1984.

Gleason, Mildred S. Caddo: A Survey of Caddo Indians in Northeast Texas and Marion County 1541-1840. Jefferson: Marion County Historical Commission, 1981.

Bibliography

Goc, Michael J. Hero of the Red River, The Life and Times of Joseph Bailey. Friendship: New Past Press, 2007.

Gould, E.W. Fifty Years on the Mississippi. St. Louis: Nixon-Jones Printing, 1889.

Guthrie, Keith. Texas Forgotten Ports, Vol. II. Austin: Eakin Press, 1993.

Halbert, H.S.; and Ball, T.H. The Creek War of 1813 and 1814. Chicago: Donohue & Henneberry, 1895.

Hoffman, Wickham. Camp Court and Seige. New York: Harper & Brothers, 1877.

Humphreys, Hubert Davis. North Louisiana, Volume One: To 1865, Essays on the Region and Its History. Ruston: McGinty Trust Fund Publications, 1984.

Hunter, Louis C. Steamboats on the Western Rivers: An Economic and Technological History. Mineola: Courier Dover Publications, 1994.

Johnson, Leland R. The Falls City Engineers - A History of the Louisville District Corps of Engineers United States Army. Washington: U.S. Army Corps of Engineers, 1974.

Kelman, Ari. A River and Its City: The Nature of Landscape in New Orleans. Berkeley: University of California Press, 2006.

Latrobe, Charles Joseph. The Rambler in North America. London: R.B. Seeley & W. Burnside, 1835.

Moran, Nathan K. Earthquakes: Myths and Social Impacts. Memphis: The University of Memphis Press, 2008.

O'Pry, Maude Hearn. Chronicles of Shreveport and Caddo Parish. Shreveport: Journal Print Company, 1928.

Shallat, Todd A. Structures in the Stream: Water, Science, and the Rise of the U.S. Army Corps of Engineers. Austin, University of Texas Press, 1994.

Smith, Steven D.; and Castille, George J. III. Bailey's Dam. Baton Rouge: Louisiana Archeological Survey and Antiquities Commission, 1986.

Southern Publishing Company. Biographical and Historical Memoirs of Northwest Louisiana. Chicago: Southern Publishing Company, 1890.

Swanton, John R. Source Material on the History and Ethnology of the Caddo Indians. Norman: University of Oklahoma Press, 1996.

Tucker, Spencer. Blue & Gray Navies: The Civil War Afloat. Annapolis: Naval Institute Press, 2006.

Villiers du Terrage, Marc de. An Explorer of Louisiana: Jean-Baptiste Bénard de la Harpe. Arkadelphia: Institute for Regional Studies, Ouachita Baptist University, 1983.

Wedel, Mildred Mott. La Harpe's 1719 Post on Red River and Nearby Caddo Settlements. Austin: Texas Memorial Museum, 1978.

Bibliography

Whayne, Jeannie M.; and Williams, Nancy A. <u>Arkansas Biography: A Collection of Notable Lives.</u> Fayetteville: University of Arkansas Press, 2000.

Wilkerson, Lyn. <u>Roads Less Traveled.</u> Bloomington: iUniverse, 2000.

Bibliography – Periodicals Cited

"Removal of the Red River Raft." Daily Picayune. 18 November 1841.

"The Red River Raft." The Manufacturer and Builder, Vol. IV, No. 1. January 1872.

"The Removal of the Red River Raft". The New York Times. 30 August 1873.

Army Corps of Engineers, Tulsa District. "Flash from the Past." Tulsa District Record. March/April 2001.

Berry, Trey. "The Expedition of William Dunbar and George Hunter along the Ouachita River, 1804-1805." Arkansas Historical Quarterly. 1 January 2003.

Caldwell, Norman W. "The Red River Raft." Chronicles of Oklahoma, Vol. 19, No. 3. September 1941.

Cox, Isaac Joslin, "The Louisiana-Texas Frontier III." Southwestern Historical Quarterly, Vol. 17, No. 2. October, 1913.

Cox, Isaac Joslin. "The Freeman Red River Expedition." Proceedings of the American Philosophical Society, Vol. 92, No. 2, Studies of Historical Documents in the Library of the American Philosophical Society. 5 May 1948.

DeBow, J.D.B. "Red River Raft." Debow's Review Vol. XXVI. - Third Series, Vol. I. 1859.

Bibliography

DeBow, J.D.B., "Red River Raft Again." Debow's Review Vol. XXI. - Third Series, Vol. I. 1856.

DeBow, J.D.B., "Red River Raft." Debow's Review Vol. XIX. - New Series, Vol. II. 1855.

Dorsey, Florence L. "Of Shreve & the River." Time Magazine. 27 October 1941.

Glover, William B. "A History of the Caddo Indians." The Louisiana Historical Quarterly, Vol. 18, No. 4. October 1935.

Grondine, E.P. "Everything is Connected: Searching for Historical Impacts in North America and a Survey of Southern and Eastern Native American Sites." Cambridge Conference Correspondence. 4 September 2000.

Hardin, J. Fair. "Henry Miller Shreve." Louisiana Historical Quarterly. Vol. 10, No. 1. January 1927.

Herbert, P.O. "The Red River Raft." Washington Telegraph. 18 March 1846.

McCall, Edith. "The Attack on the Great Raft." American Heritage Magazine. Volume 3, Issue 3. Winter 1988.

Northrop, E.B.; Chittenden, H.A.; and Bishop, W.H. "The Red River Raft." The Wisconsin Lumberman. 1873.

Smith, Ralph A. "Account of the Journey of Benard de La Harpe: Discovery Made by Him of Several Nations Situated in the West." Southwestern Historical Quarterly, Vol. 62. July, 1958.

Bibliography – Online Resources Cited

Louisiana Naval War Commission. "Louisiana's Military Heritage: Battles, Campaigns, and Maneuvers." 2006. <http://www.usskidd.com/battles-redriver.html>.

Muncrief, Dennis. "The Great Red River Raft." Oklahoma Genealogy & History. 5 January 2005. <www.okgenweb.org/~okmurray/Murray/stories/great_red_river_raft.htm>.

U.S. Geological Survey. "The Mississippi Valley – Whole Lotta Shakin' Goin' On." <http://quakes.usgs.gov/prepare/factsheets/NewMadrid>.

Bibliography – Government Resources Cited

"Certificate of power of attorney from the Caddo Indians to Jehiel Brooks, September 13, 1836," The Brooks-Queen Family Collection, American Catholic History Research Center and University Archives, Catholic University of America, Washington, D.C.

"Extracts from various letters relating to Jehiel Brooks' duties as an Indian Agent and Caddo Indians Lands, February 28, 1832 – August 19, 1835." The Brooks-Queen Family Collection, American Catholic History Research Center and University Archives, Catholic University of America, Washington, D.C.

30th. Cong., 1st. sess., Ex. Doc., Vol. V, No. 49. Washington: 1849.

Abert, Colonel J.J. Report to Congress, November 1, 1845, 29th. Cong., 1st, sess., Sen. Doc., Vol. III, No. 26. Washington, 1845.

Abert, Colonel J.J. Report to Congress, November 14, 1860, 36th Congress, Sen. Doc., Vol. II, No. 1. Washington: 1860.

Abert, Colonel J.J. Report to Congress, November 15, 1844, 28th Cong., 2nd sess., Sen. Doc., Vol. I, No. 1. Washington, 1844.

Abert, Colonel J.J. <u>Report to Secretary Davis, 03/15/1856, 34th Congress, 1st Session, Sen. Ex. Doc., Vol. XII, No. 49.</u> Washington: 1856.

Constitution of the Confederate States of America, as adopted on March 11, 1861, Article 1, Section 8, Paragraph 3.

DeSoto Parish, Louisiana 1850 Federal Census.

Fuller, Charles A. <u>Annual Report to Congress, September 1, 1855, 34th Congress, 1st and 2nd Session, Sen. Doc., Vol. ii, No. 1.</u> Washington: 1855.

<u>Red River Survey, 01/18-02/17/1855, 33rd Congress, 2nd Session, Sen. Ex. Doc., Vol. iii, No. 62.</u> Washington: 1855.

<u>Reports From the Court of Claims Submitted to the House of Representatives During the First Session of the Thirty-Sixth Congress, 1859-1860.</u> Washington: C. Wendell, 1860.

U.S. Army Corps of Engineers, <u>Red River Waterway Project Shreveport, LA, to Daingerfield, TX, Reevaluation Study In-Progress Review.</u> Washington: U.S. Army Corps of Engineers, 1992.

U.S. War Department. <u>Annual Report of the Secretary of War.</u> Washington: U.S. Govt. Printing Office, 1874.

Woodruff, A.E. <u>Report of the Chief of Engineers, October 19, 1872, 42nd Congress, 3rd SessionEx. Doc. No.1, Pt. 2, Vol. II.</u> Washington: U.S. Army Corps of Engineers, 1872.

Index

Abert, Colonel, 71
Adams, President John Quincy, 58
Aid, The, 88
Alexandria Rapids, 16, 78
Alexandria, Louisiana, 12, 16, 76, 83
Allegheny Mountains, 53
American Philosophical Society, 35
Archimedes, The, 66
Arkadelphia, Arkansas, 30
Arkansas River, 28
Atchafalaya, 76
Bailey, Lieutenant Colonel Joseph, 84
Banks, General N.P., 82
Bayou Pierre, 27, 62, 84
Bayou Wallace, 49
Bellefontaine Cemetery, 68
Bennett, William S., 61
Bienville, Jean-Baptiste Le Moyne, 22
Bistmon Lake, 12
Black Bayou, 90
Black Hawk, The, 64
Black River, 28, 29
Bodeau Lake, 12
Boone, Daniel, 59
Boston, Massachusetts, 7
Bowman, A.H., 64

Brazos River, 50
Brooks, Jehiel, 43, 44, 45, 47, 49, 61
Broutin, J.F., 10
Caddo Indians, 6, 16, 38, 41, 62
Caddo Lake, 77
Caddo Parish, Louisiana, 50
Calfait Creek, 31
Camden, Arkansas, 29
Cane River, 10
Cane, James H., 61
Carter, Walker Randolph, 68
Cass, Lewis, 52, 61
Charleston, South Carolina, 8
Chickasaw Bluffs, 14
Civil War, 81
Coashutta Indians, 38
Coles Creek culture, 11
Comanche Indians, 50
Company of the Indies, 10, 22
Confederate Constitution, 81
Corn Dance, 49
Cornett, Ed, 51
Cox, Isaac Joslin, 35
Cumberland River, 14

Custis, Dr. Peter, 34
Cypress Bayou, 49
Daily Picayune, The, 69
Dauphin Island, 22
DeBow, James Dunwoody Brownson, 75
DeBow's Review, 12, 75
Des Moines, Iowa, 54
DeSoto Parish, Louisiana, 72
Dewees, W.B., 13
Dooley's Bayou, 74, 79
Dunbar, William, 26
Dunbar-Hunter Expedition, 26
Dutch John's Lake, 78
E.A. Woodruff, The, 92
Edwards, John, 62
Edwards, Larkin, 46, 49, 61, 63
Ellicott, Andrew, 34
Ellis, N.D., 79
Emerald Park, 24
Enterprise, The, 56
Eradicator, The, 64, 69, 70
Flint, Timothy, 18
Florida War, 73
Fort Adams, 34
Fort Miro, 28, 32
Fort Saint Louis de los Cadodaquious, 23
Freeman, Thomas, 5, 34, 36, 52, 92
Freeman-Custis Expedition, 10, 34, 42

French, Daniel, 56
Fuller, Charles A., 73
Fulton, Robert, 15, 56, 67
Fulton-Livingston Company, 56, 57
Gilmer, James B., 79
Grand Expedition, 32
Grappé, Francois, 61, 62
Gratiot, Brigadier General, 52
Great Comet of 1811, 55
Great Track, Chief, 27
Grondine, E.P., 10
Habberton, John, 19
Heliopolis, The, 60, 66
Henry M. Shreve, The, 65
Herring, Judge E., 44
Hervey, C.M., 79
Hotchkiss, T.P., 79
Howard Association, The, 91
Howell, C.W., 88, 91
Humphrey, Lieutenant, 34
Hunter, Dr. George, 27
impact event, 10
Jackson, President Andrew, 50, 56
Jefferson, President Thomas, 26, 32, 38
Jefferson, Texas, 74, 82
Jenkins, Bushrod, 61
John Davis, Captain John, 8
Kalbaugh, The, 89
Kianeche River, 79
King Philip V, 21

Index

La Harpe, Jean-Baptiste Bénard, 10, 21
Lafitte, Pirate Brothers, 54
Landrum, John M., 79
Latrobe, Charles Joseph, 55
Laurel, The, 64
Law, John, 22
Lewis and Clark Expedition, 26, 32, 40
Lincoln, President Abraham, 82
Linnard, T.B., 70
Little Rock, Arkansas, 24
Loggy Bayou, 12, 82
Long Prairie, 17
Louisiana Purchase, 26, 27, 32
Louisiana, Arkansas, and Texas Navigation Company, 79
Louisville, Kentucky, 56
Malvern, Arkansas, 31
Mansfield, Louisiana, 83
Marietta, Ohio, 57
McNeil, Angus, 61
Mexican-American War, 71
Mississippi River, 8, 12, 14, 22, 53, 56, 60, 66, 76, 79
Missouri River, 26
Monongahela River, 52
Monroe, Louisiana, 28
Mound Prairie, 18
Nacogdoches, Texas, 37
Nashville, Tennessee, 14
Nassonites Indians, 23
Natchez under the hill, 15
Natchez, Mississippi, 8, 14, 26, 32
Natchitoches, Louisiana, 10, 12, 16, 18, 34, 35, 39, 60, 82
Neighbors, Robert S., 50
New Falls City, The, 82, 83
New Madrid Earthquake, 7, 10
New Madrid, Missouri, 10
New Orleans Gazette, 32
New Orleans, Louisiana, 22, 24, 32, 54, 56, 75, 86, 90
New Orleans, The, 56
New York Times, The, 89, 90
New York, New York, 32
Nick Biddle, The, 63
Oakland Cemetery, 92
Ohio River, 14, 53, 55, 57, 60, 73
Osage Indians, 27
Ouachita Indians, 35
Ouachita Post, 28
Ouachita River, 28, 29, 30, 33
Our Country, 19
Pascagoula Bayou, 49, 62
Peach Orchard Bluff, 46, 49
Pearl, The, 64

Philadelphia, Pennsylvania, 12, 32, 53, 54
Pickett, James B., 61
Pittsburgh, Pennsylvania, 28, 56
Pleasant Hill, Louisiana, 83
Polk, President James, 72
Porter, Admiral D.D., 82
Quapaw Indians, 42
Red River, 15, 22, 27, 28, 33, 34, 41, 49, 51, 52, 60, 62, 69, 73, 75, 82
Red River Campaign, 82
Republic of Texas, 50
Revenue, The, 64
Richter Scale, 7
Rio Grande River, 82
River and Harbor Act, 88
Rokafull, Dona Maria, 21
Romance of California Life, 19
Rusk, General, 50
Sabine River, 49
Sac and Fox Indians, 54
Saint-Malo, France, 21, 22, 25
San Francisco Earthquake, 7
Sanders, John, 73
Seawell, Lieutenant W., 52
Shreve Town Company, 61, 69
Shreve, Henry Miller, 12, 52, 59, 61, 68, 69, 89
Shreve, Isaiah, 52

Shreve, Mary, 52
Shreveport, Louisiana, 50, 63, 64, 74, 79, 82, 83, 90
Sibley, John, 34
Soda Lake, 74, 79
Sparks, Captain Richard, 34
Sprague, Sturges, 61
Springfield Landing, 82
St. Catherine's Landing, 28
St. Louis, Missouri, 53, 68
Sterling, The, 90
Sulphur River, 22
Tarshar, Chief, 46, 48, 62
Thoreau, Henry David, 19
Touline, M., 37
Troyville culture, 11
Tsauninot, Underchief, 46, 47, 62
Twelve Mile Bayou, 42, 74
Tyler, President John, 65
U.S. Army Corps of Engineers, 61, 69, 71, 84, 88
U.S. Geological Survey, 8
United States Military Academy, 73
University of Louisiana, 75
Van Winkle, Rip, 13
Viana, Don Francisco, 38, 39
Walnut Hills, 14
War of the Quadruple Alliance, 23
Washington, D.C., 8
Washington, The, 57

Index

Washita River, 51
Wheeling, West Virginia, 57
Whig Party, 65
White Oak Shoals, 13
Williamson, Thomas Taylor, 61, 69, 72
Wisconsin Lumberman, The, 89
Woodruff, Eugene Augustus, 88
Woodruff, George, 92
Youghiogheny River, 52

CPSIA information can be obtained at www.ICGtesting.com
Printed in the USA
LVOW10s0506270816

501995LV00001B/10/P